COMIC CON
CHRISTIANITY

COMIC CON
CHRISTIANITY

JEN SCHLAMEUSS-PERRY

Paulist Press
New York / Mahwah, NJ

Cover art by Sharon West
Cover design by Joe Gallagher
Book design by Sharyn Banks

Library of Congress Cataloging-in-Publication Data is available upon request.

ISBN 978-0-8091-5370-1 (paperback)
ISBN 978-1-58768-743-3 (e-book)

Published by Paulist Press
997 Macarthur Boulevard
Mahwah, New Jersey 07430

www.paulistpress.com

Printed and bound in the
United States of America

To the Sisters Filippini and the Jesuits,
who trained me in faith
and helped me form my spiritual imagination,
sense of justice,
and understanding of
who I am as a child of God

CONTENTS

ACKNOWLEDGMENTS

This book happened because of the care and support of many who were heroes to me. The only way I can possibly think to thank everyone is in chronological order. First, my parents: Dad, who introduced me to so much of the fandom that has become part of me, and Mom, who always encouraged me to write. My grandma, Elsie Schlameuss, while she was on this Earth, tried very hard to encourage me to develop ladylike pursuits, and I learned that if there's one thing a proper lady can do, it's write letters. She went out of her way to get me to write, and it's actually come in handy at work, and definitely helped my writing overall. My teachers, especially Kevin C. Houtz and Helen M. Bryce, who gave me my start in writing, were wonderful mentors. Allison Barron, in her gentleness, taught me how to be edited. Saint Anthony answered a very off-the-cuff prayer and set this whole thing in motion. I offer a most heartfelt thank you to my amazing editor, Christopher Bellitto, who championed the book and made it better than it ever would have been if I was left to my own devices, and his lovely wife and daughter who helped read. Thank you to the folks at Paulist Press who took a chance on me and my book. Thank you to Master Sue Kalinski Hinkelbein for teaching me self-confidence on a ton of different levels. Thank you to my boss and colleagues at the Co-Cathedral of St. Robert Bellarmine in New Jersey, as well as the fabulous parishioners there for their moral support, enthusiastic encouragement, and prayers. Thank you to my siblings, in-laws, especially my mother-in-law, and out-laws for their support.

My husband, Ken, and our sons, Benjamin and Nathaniel, have been awesome throughout my writing, putting up with me on my computer during family time, doing "research" with me by watching movies and cartoons, and not getting offended when I periodically lost it. You guys are the best and I love you.

INTRODUCTION

Which Hero Are You?

The Power of Story

Heroes rock. They have permeated the storytelling of every culture for at least as long as stories have been recorded. Monsters and villains, threats to the livelihood and well-being of society, have always been a problem and heroes have always been the answer. Throughout human history, stories of heroes have been crucial to the development of cultures, morality, and teaching. Some of the earliest (and best) literature that we know of contains hero stories. The Book of Genesis references the "heroes of old," the Nephilim, and then takes off running with hero after hero saving God's people. Every generation had its heroes, from Beowulf to Siegfried to King Arthur, with our more recent heroes given us by J.R.R. Tolkien, C. S. Lewis, Stan Lee, Gene Roddenberry, and countless others. Our hero stories can inform our faith and help us to understand the principles of Christianity on a deeper level. It would be foolish to ignore the opportunity to learn from the stories that we love.

While I have no interest in christening stories that aren't intentionally faith based, I do have an interest in introducing them to one another. You see, I'm a yenta at heart (Yiddish for matchmaker), and I love bringing people together who I think would enjoy one another's company. My religious imagination grew up alongside my literary one, and they have been excellent company for one another ever since. This book isn't meant to be deep theology, nor is it meant to be a definitive work on nerd culture. I mean for it to be an opening dialogue between two cultures that I love, and an entertaining look at each for those who already love them both as I do.

God continually used storytelling to facilitate our unfolding religious understanding. Stories engage our intellect and imagination. They inspire and challenge us to relate to them and find deeper meaning. Carrying on the tradition of self-revelation that God began through the stories of the Hebrew Scriptures, Jesus did most of his teaching through storytelling, and then the evangelists revealed Jesus to us through their stories about him. Jesus adapted the objects of his stories to the subjects in the crowd. He told stories of the most unlikely heroes and equally unlikely villains. In fact, when he began a story, you didn't know who the hero was going to be until the end, and it was often shocking. His listeners recognized themselves in his characters; his stories challenged their assumptions and inspired them to change the way they lived.

Some of the most ancient hero stories include the giant Nephilim, who were the result of fallen angel/human relationships (Gen 6:1–4). They're mentioned in passing, which assumes that the reader is familiar with them. They are discussed in slightly greater detail in the Book of Enoch, and they seem to be referred to as the Philistines and the giants found in Canaan in the early history of Israel. One of the Christian letters in the Bible, the Letter of Jude, mentions them, too, regarding how they led humans astray and would be judged for it. Besides the Nephilim, Genesis gives us the sea monsters (Gen 1:21) that live in the great bodies of water, and both the Bible and Mesopotamian culture share the story of Noah or Gilgamesh, respectively, who with divine help survive a flood that wipes out every living thing on the planet. They were good when everyone else was bad, and it was up to them to restart the planet. The ancients also gave us the awesome Greek and Egyptian myths with gods and demigods, whose stories are still being told and reworked today.

From the Middle Ages, we're gifted with hero stories like *Beowulf*. Grendel, Beowulf's foe, is a nasty devil-spawned monster who lives under a fiery lake and raids the mead hall of King Hrothgar, stealing men, ripping their arms off, and eating them. Beowulf, a fearless hero with superhuman strength who can hold his breath for a super long time, dives into that fiery lake and goes after and defeats Grendel. Of course, this makes his monster mom mad and then Beowulf must fight her, too.

The medieval bards offered wonderful stories of valiant knights, like Ivanhoe, Sir Gawain, and King Arthur. One of the oldest is the story of Siegfried, a Germanic demigod who reforged his father's famous sword, Nothung (or Gram if you're going by the *Volsunga Saga*), which has since appeared in the cartoon Adventure Time and many video games. It was borrowed and renamed by Tolkien to tell the story of Narsil; when reforged, it would become Aragorn's sword. Siegfried used Nothung to kill the dragon, Fafnir, and then gained invincibility by bathing in its blood (after a little birdie told him to) and had a cloak that made him invisible (not unlike Harry Potter's gift from his father or a certain Ring that makes its Middle-earth wearers invisible).

He has many interesting adventures and was so cool that he got his own opera, which was even featured in Bugs Bunny cartoons.

We have our modern-day comic book heroes (some of whom are based on the ancient stories); we still can't get enough of monsters and villains, and the amazing guys and girls who defeat them. Now, as much as ever, we *need* hero stories. The world seems to be going completely nuts; there is so much pain, injustice, and terror. Our brains need a break. Our hearts need to be inspired. We need to see powerful people using their power for the good of others, instead of for their own gain at the expense of the already weak. We need our faith in humanity restored.

Let's take a real-life example. After a day filled with news updates flashing across my cellphone heralding disaster after disaster, I plopped on my couch and caught the end of an episode of *Star Trek: The Next Generation* that my boys were watching. Will Riker had just, very bravely, stood up to an old commander of his who wanted to do something wrong. Don't ask me what—I missed it. In a past assignment, this same commander led Will into some treaty-breaking activity against the Romulans. This business was found out and both the commander and Will were going to have to face trial with the Federation. Captain Picard told his "Number One" how proud of him he was for doing the right thing in the current situation, and for being truthful about the wrong he had done in the past. Will didn't try to get out of it—he was determined to accept whatever repercussions his actions would have, even though, at the time, he was very young and was just following orders.

The fatherly interaction between Picard and Number One, the courage Will displayed in standing up to his superior who was in error, and the honor he carried with him while he was uncertain of his future made me glad that my sons were watching. It wasn't just because they had chosen to watch *Star Trek* when I wasn't in control of the remote, but because they were seeing men in authority behaving well. I hope that I'm raising young men who will grow to be leaders in whatever situation they find themselves, and it heartens me that if they should find themselves in a sticky one, they might (even if it's subconsciously) have the example of Jean-Luc Picard and Will Riker in their arsenal of responses.

Naturally, they have actual, living human beings in their lives as examples, too. But kind of like godparents, fictional characters are people who aren't the parents that we *must* listen to; they're like cool aunts and uncles whom we look up to, who share our family's values, and who help to teach us a right way to live by the example of their lives.

Superpowers for Everyone!

Many heroes come from a far-off land or even another planet. They offer hope unlooked for, freedom from dangers too big for us to handle, and an image of what greatness looks like; and they unlock something in us that makes us want to aspire to greatness, too. Hero stories invite us to believe in the impossible and to invest in it. Men and women who can fly, or lift any weight, or run faster than fast; people who can travel through time and space, go invisible, read our thoughts, change their shape—even people who can absorb (or steal) other heroes' powers—there's something in us that wants to believe that those things are possible. We become invested (admit it) on a sort of a strange level in the most minute details. Heated arguments on physics, canon, and logic break out when even the most amiable of people start talking heroes—and not just on *The Big Bang Theory*. We will fight with the people we love and respect most in the world over our opinions, swearing on all that is good and holy that they are indisputable facts. I can be so insistent on my correctness that very few humans will engage me in an actual conversation about heroes. My children roll their eyes, my friends stare blankly, and my coworkers pray that nothing "superhero or Middle-earth" comes up at lunch (but smile and nod politely when it inevitably does).

And, who among us hasn't been waiting for *that* moment—the moment that the gamma rays hit you, or the spider bites you, or some random mutation takes shape, or the Force finally kicks in, or the TARDIS lands; because it would be enough just to be a Companion even if you can't be a Time Lord, yourself. From the time we were old enough to ask our moms to fasten a towel or our blanky around our necks to make a cape, we've been pretending to be the heroes we most looked up to. Who among us doesn't think that, in the right situation, with the right circumstances, we could be a hero, too?

This is the power that stories hold for us; they have the power to change people who can change the world. Whether the stories are from the Bible, sci-fi, comics, or video games, the heroes they introduce us to have the ability to reshape generations. God knows better than to give me actual superpowers, but God also arranged life so that it doesn't take superpowers to do amazing things. All of us are called to greatness; we just have to live God's call to us.

Heroes challenge us to access truth in the stories—the truth that justice is more important than fear, that selfless giving is more honorable than protecting your own life, that our human values are worth defending even against insurmountable odds, and that *we can win*.

These stories necessarily have a moral and spiritual quality to them because they deal with the struggle between good and evil. And they resound with us because we live that struggle every day. We may not have to fight alien forces or corrupt rich guys who have access to ridiculous tech (although that's looking more likely every day); but we do face injustice, isolation, and the degradation of core human values and dignity. Every. Single. Day. Many of us live in mediocrity; not offering much to the people around us, not feeling fulfilled, not doing too much that's very interesting at all. We battle boredom and irrelevance. It would be cool to have an adventure. It would be cool to make a radical difference. It would be cool to discover that there is something uniquely remarkable about us—something of substance.

The values and attributes we appreciate in our heroes are the same values and attributes that we find in God. Uncompromising justice, self-emptying service to humanity, the protection of and preferential option for the poor, marginalized, and defenseless, healing the brokenhearted and downtrodden, having the ability to enslave the world with no trouble but choosing to promote true freedom instead—these are attributes of God; these are attributes of heroes.

Amazingly, they're our attributes, too, because we're made in the image and likeness of God. Besides that, God told us repeatedly in the Bible that those hero activities are our mission. The prophets in the Hebrew Scriptures equate justice with caring for the widow, orphan, and alien (see Deut 10:18–20), who were the most vulnerable people in ancient society. Jesus affirms this teaching both with his words and his relationships. He spent his time with the people that were most in need of healing, attention, and affirmation. He taught that to love God was to love your neighbor as you love yourself. He went so far as to say that we should love others the way that Jesus loved us—to death. He said, "I give you a new commandment, that you love one another. Just as I have loved you, you also should love one another. By this everyone will know that you are my disciples, if you have love for one another" (John 13:34–35). The way that he showed his love for us was to sacrifice his life to save us. That's what he's referring to when he says, "As I have loved you, you should love one another."

If we chose it, we can sluff off mediocrity. No one has to live feeling irrelevant. Living for others and serving the poor and defenseless gives purpose and fulfillment; not to mention the gift of uplifting the dignity of the one to whom you reached out. Making someone who is routinely overlooked—who might feel like they have the superpower of invisibility, but wish they didn't—feel seen, feel known, gives meaning and purpose to their life, too. But we don't just go around declaring ourselves to be heroes, even if we choose to live as one in our everyday lives. And it would be best for everyone if we don't walk around wearing capes, or tights, or our underwear on the outside. In fact, Arthur from the comic book series The Tick got fired from his job in an accounting firm for wearing a moth costume that he found. His coworkers "found this kind of rampant individuality very disturbing." So would most of our employers...and families...and anyone we want to be seen in public with. The business advice that recommends you dress for the job you want doesn't really apply to superheroes. We're in good company, though; almost everyone in the pantheon of heroes has a mild-mannered alter ego. They had very normal jobs contributing to society quietly, while keeping their hero nature hidden just beneath.

God-Hero

We find a similar story in the person of Jesus. Christians believe that he is God—all-powerful, all-knowing, perfect, and eternal. He chose to come to Earth to live as the most vulnerable of us so that we could know what true power is. He came and mentored us so that we could know what true freedom is. He came and healed us so that we could carry on the work that he did and share in the abilities that he has.

While Jesus never "lost" his power, knowledge, authority, or ability, he put them aside at times to have an authentically human experience. And, by giving up his life for us on the cross, by sacrificing himself as a blameless victim for the evil we had done (and continue to do), he offered us everything that he had. By doing this, too, he gained it all back in spades:

> Though he was in the form of God, / did not regard equality with God / as something to be exploited, / but emptied himself, / taking the form of a slave, / being born in human likeness. / And being found in human form, / he humbled himself and became obedient to the point of death— / even death on a cross.
>
> Therefore God also highly exalted him / and gave him the name / that is above every name, / so that at the name of Jesus / every knee should bend, / in heaven and

on earth and under the earth, / and every tongue should confess / that Jesus Christ is Lord, / to the glory of God the Father. (Phil 2:6–11)

Our heroes, who could crush us like bugs, instead spend their energy raising up humanity and challenging us to be better. They sometimes struggle with the fact that the energy they're putting forth seems to be coming to nothing—on vast levels, the people that they serve and protect squander the freedom and safety that they're repeatedly given. The hero could easily force everyone to behave the way they want, but, like God, they continually turn their trust back over to the freewill of humanity. For example, Superman, who is essentially invincible (unless you have access to kryptonite), puts himself between humanity and every alien or homegrown evil that threatens us. Frankly, it would take way less energy to subject the world to his authority than it would to protect us from others. He would still have to fight off potential conquerors, but he wouldn't have to worry about keeping us safe in the meantime. Collateral damage could include people, and that would be a much easier fight. But when Superman is defending us, he's looking to save every guy who falls off a building, every baby whose stroller is about to have a car flip onto it. Every life has value for him, and he has offered, on many occasions, to give his life up to save one of ours. Though he proves himself to be our champion time after time, the citizens of the world treat him with suspicion and waste what he wins for us by continuing to oppress one another.

Heroes are continually disappointed, but they keep handing the freedom they win for us right back. They never give up on humanity—even when supervillains are taunting them about their silly devotion to the human race and point out that they could squash us like bugs. The heroes' care for the weak and broken, flawed and corrupt people of Earth is very much reflective of what is expressed in the Bible about God's relationship with us. God never gives up on us and never takes our freedom away, no matter how badly we abuse it. He laments our misuse of, frankly, everything he gives us, but continues to put himself out there so that we can try again.

The prophet Hosea offers us a wonderful image to express this. In his story, God tells Hosea to take his cheating wife, Gomer, back into his house after she's been all around the block with no regard for him or his children. Hosea and Gomer represent the relationship between God and Israel. The people of Israel were in an almost chronic state of worshiping other gods, which is symbolized by marital infidelity. When Israel wanders off with other gods, our God's plan is, "I will now allure her, / and bring her into the wilderness, / and speak tenderly to her" (Hos 2:14). And, after they work on their relationship a little, God promises, "I will take you for my wife forever; I will take you for my wife in righteousness and in justice, in steadfast love, and in mercy. I will take you for my wife in faithfulness; and you shall know the LORD" (Hos 2:19–20). God knows Israel will stray again. God knows we will. But God continually takes us back, speaking tenderly; gently wooing, and always forgiving. Now, that's love.

There's even a sense that our weakness is somehow endearing to him—it's something to be protected, not destroyed. "For while we were still weak, at the right time Christ died for the ungodly. Indeed, rarely will anyone die for a righteous person—though perhaps for a good person someone might actually dare to die. But God proves his love for us in that while we still were sinners Christ died for us" (Rom 5:6–8).

I see this quality in many of the heroes I love. Doctor Who pops right into my mind with his consistent declaration that Earth is protected by him. In episode upon episode, The Doctor is disappointed with humanity's fear and weakness. We try to solve every problem with weapons because of our fear. Both UNIT and Torchwood, organizations set up to learn about and protect the Earth from aliens, treat The Doctor as a potential threat, but also look for his help when the world is in trouble. Whether it's due to the individual humans he grew to love, or the general potential he sees in humanity, The Doctor has made it his business to protect the Earth from all kinds of alien villains. The companions he takes in the TARDIS, flawed as they are, keep him grounded, compassionate, and in touch with reality. He sees humanity at its worst and its best, and emboldens us to take risks that will save others, just as he does for us.

It Is Your Destiny

As Christians, we're told that we should imitate Christ and become like him. It's not meant to be symbolic. That's right, we can share in the abilities that Jesus had—he even told us that we'd do *greater* things than him; "the one who believes in me will also do the works that I do and, in fact, will do greater works than these, because I am going to the Father" (John 14:12).

It may sound nuts, but Christians are used to believing the impossible. We believe that God made everything out of nothing, made us in his image and likeness, loves us no matter how bad we are, became human, died, and came back to life, and that we eat the body of Christ. Really, believing in superheroes should be as natural as breathing for Christians. Believing that we can be one should be, too. We come from heroes: flawed, broken, sometimes with villainous roots; but people who did amazing things because they believed in something bigger than themselves. Paul the Apostle was a murderer, Peter the Apostle denied Jesus and left him all alone after declaring that he'd be with him till the end, Dorothy Day was a Communist and had an abortion; but they all came to know God's love and forgiveness and it moved them to uplift humanity in miraculous ways.

Our Tradition breeds us for greatness, leadership, healing, and bringing justice to the downtrodden. We are told that if we live an authentic relationship with God, we can change the world, complete the mission of Christ, and bring about perfect justice. If we all live the vocation—the destiny that God has determined for us in our baptism—we could make the superheroes that we all want to believe in real.

If you were brought up on superheroes and sci-fi, and if you were brought up Catholic, then you probably have an excellent understanding of destiny. You knew from an early age, or at least suspected, that there is something special about *you*, and that you have a particular role to fulfill in this life. You were born for something great.

Every hero knows, sometimes from within and sometimes because they were told, that there's something that they, and they alone, must do for the salvation of the planet. Superman, Luke Skywalker, the various Green Lanterns, Spiderman—pick a hero—they have an understanding that the power they have been given saddles them with a responsibility to change the course of history. They didn't just grab their tights and go for it, though. They struggled; hung out in quiet solitude; engaged in a discernment process, intense martial arts, or Jedi training with people of better understanding; and let their calling grow in them until they were ready to find their opportunity to strike out in faith. There were never any guarantees of success, but that's where faith comes in; faith that if they do what they can to the best of their abilities, they can contribute to a mission much bigger than themselves, and while they might not defeat the villain entirely, they can make a dent for others to keep hacking away at.

Paul the Apostle had an experience like this. Paul was a highly educated Pharisee, a doctor of Jewish law, who felt a strong obligation to wipe out Christianity. He believed that they were blaspheming and made it his mission to protect orthodoxy in Judaism. He had loads of Christians arrested and killed. He was even present for the first Christian martyrdom when Stephen was stoned to death. While he was on his way to wipe out a large Christian community, Jesus approached him, knocked him on his bottom, and asked, "Saul, Saul, why do you persecute me?" (Acts 9:4). Paul was named Saul at the time. When Paul (Saul) got up, he was temporarily blind. Jesus sent him to Damascus, where he would meet a guy named Ananias (not the one from Paul's trial in Jerusalem). Jesus told Ananias that Paul was coming and to welcome and heal him. Ananias wasn't happy with this order, because everyone knew who Saul (Paul) was and what he had been up to. The community didn't take an immediate shine to him. Everyone was afraid that he was there to infiltrate and kill them, too. But they listened to Jesus. They put their fear aside and welcomed their enemy, healed him, and taught him all about Jesus. Paul was converted and God changed his name from Saul to Paul (God does that sometimes). Through his encounter with Christ, and then more deeply through the

Christian community's faith and trust in God, Paul became the single most important apostle of the Gospel. Before he went out to share what he learned, though, he spent years being formed in the faith. It was his destiny, but it took a windy road, getting knocked on his butt, and many years of preparation before he was ready to live it out.

If you're a Christian, you were told that, like Paul, you also have a destiny. You were told this first through your baptism, and then your teachers fleshed it out for you. In the Catholic baptism ritual, we are anointed to be priest, prophet, and king because that's who Jesus was, and we're baptized into his mission. We are pretty much born into it, and even live it as babies because we are reflections of God's love just by *being*, but it takes a good long time for the meaning of our baptismal destiny to unfold; maybe even a whole lifetime. We need struggle, solitude, discernment, and opportunity to be ready to live it.

On one hand, as Christians, we share the same destiny, and on the other hand, in our uniqueness, we all have individual destinies. To be priest is to minister to everyone God puts in front of us—to care for their needs, to pray for them, to sacrifice ourselves for them. The way any individual might live this out differs. Parents, police, ordained priests, and physical therapists care for, root for, pray for, and sacrifice for the people they serve. To be a prophet is to speak the Word of God to everyone who needs good news. Parents, police, ordained priests, and physical therapists speak the truth in love—and those things originate in God—so we speak God's own words to others. To be a king we need only to be God's kids. To be God's kids means that we live in real freedom—actual freedom. We have absolutely nothing to be afraid of if we're partnering with God. Bad stuff will still happen, but since we belong to God, we'll always have the strength and healing to accomplish whatever work God has for us. Being a king means that we inherit heaven with Jesus. That's every Christian's basic destiny.

The specific gifts that God gives to each one of us, and how we choose to use them, determines our destiny. It could be to be a parent, or a teacher, or a friend, or a sanitation engineer, or a soldier, or a ninja...or anything. It could be a lot of different things over time. It could make the difference in someone's life because of a moment of kindness and dignity that you offered to them. But it's all service. It's all sacrifice. It's all ministry. And it's what we're all called to. It is our destiny.

Ready for Excitement and Adventure

While we all want some excitement and adventure, we often shrink back from taking the risks that provide them. There are plenty of risks in everyday life; we're presented with them continually. But we ignore them, delay them, and rationalize why we shouldn't engage them. That doesn't make us nonhero material. Consider how many heroes shied away from their destinies before embracing them. Frodo, Sam, Merry, and Pippin would have been beyond content to stay in the Shire forever if Middle-earth as they knew it (their tiny corner of it) wasn't being threatened by the all-seeing Eye of Sauron. Han Solo just wanted to go about his smuggling schemes. Iron Man is a naturally self-centered guy who'd rather look out just for himself and *maybe* Pepper, rather than being part of an Earth-defending team where he would have to rely on others. Aquaman (who doesn't get enough props) preferred to hang out with his fishy friends and defend his ocean home, rather than get mucked up with the land-dwellers who caused most of his problems.

If we were to make categories of heroes, there's a whole big one for "reluctant heroes." Start making a list in your head... most of them, right? It usually takes the Earth on the very edge of obliteration or the person they love the most finding themselves in some terrible danger (probably being abducted by the villain while he taunts the hero) to make them finally launch into action. So, why should you be different?

A mild-mannered mother might let small incidents involving her offspring at school or on the soccer field pass by, chalking them up to life lessons and opportunities to build character or resilience. But if she feels that her young one is the victim of injustice, then watch out, world! She will move heaven and earth to make sure that her child had the same (if not more) opportunities that every other kid gets. A kind, compassionate boy might take a lot of nonsense from his friends, but if they pick on his little brother, he will make them feel the folly of their ways.

Everyone has that *one thing* that brings out their protective nature; the thing that means so much to them that they won't just sit by and let it be harmed or destroyed. Jesus calmly taught and healed people as he made his way through Israel. He was peaceful and merciful in every situation. Even when he corrected people—even when they were about to unjustly kill a woman—even when they whipped and crucified him—he corrected with kindness. But when he got to the temple and saw the abuses that were occurring, the business that had been built around "worship," he lost it. He yelled, flipped over tables, made a whip, and threw people out (see Matt 21:12-13). You can mess with him, but do *not* mess with his Dad.

So, what does it take to move us into action? There's no shortage of villains in our world. Injustice is everywhere you look. How much are we willing to take before we claim our destiny and enter a world of adventure and excitement?

Coworkers are gossiping viciously at the watercooler...take a risk and defend the one they're slandering? If you answered yes, you're in for some serious adventure, possibly very unpleasant adventure. But you'll be a hero to the slandered one. Your racist uncle is spewing offensive slurs at a gathering of your people-pleasing, peace-at-whatever-cost family...kindly engage him in a civil philosophical conversation about how all people are created in the image and likeness of God? If you answered yes, fasten your cape, because some excitement is headed right for you. And you might not get invited to family gatherings anymore. Homeless man in distress on the sidewalk while you're out with friends... stop and help him, disrupting everyone's fun, and risk being left behind? If you said yes, excitement and adventure might plummet from your life, as you might now be known as the guy who ditches dinner friends for homeless guys. But then you'll be a hero to the man whose dignity you raised and maybe whose life you saved. And, maybe it will give you room for better quality friends....

The life of a hero isn't cushy and pleasant. It's bumpy, dangerous, and sometimes lonely. When we choose to imitate our heroes, we will find destiny knocking at our door, fulfillment and relevance, and a dissipation of fear as we come to know who we are more perfectly. We can decide who we will become and what sort of legacy we want to leave behind. We can choose what kind of hero we want to be.

CHAPTER ONE

SUPER GROUPS

The Body of Christ

Community Life

Across the comic book universe, you find heroes working in teams. Many of them formed intentionally, like the Justice League, the Avengers, and the X-Men. They had a common goal, a common foe, and common needs. The Justice League started when heroes realized they couldn't defend the universe alone. They needed an organized effort to defeat the growing threats against the universe. The Avengers were formed through the intercession of S.H.I.E.L.D., a government-sponsored national security outfit. They recognized the special talents of the various heroes and invited them to work together to protect the world from specific threats. The X-Men came together as the result of a compassionate visionary who wanted to provide a safe place for heroes to live, learn, and grow together so that they could discover how to use their powers for the benefit of others. Then, there's The City. The City is not a cool group of heroes that has a central command post or a nifty group name; it's a geographical location that happens to have a plethora of folks who would be heroes living within it.

Each of these super-group systems reminds me of different ways of being Church. There are many models of community living within Christianity, and many models of Church. Each suits the needs of its demographic. Like our hero communities, some form because an authority recognizes a community in need of a parish, some form out of a common need or desire, some form as a matter of survival, and some are more free-form—kind of loosely associating with one another on projects and missions. Each is a legitimate way of being community and each serves a purpose for the individuals involved.

One of the many phrases for expressing the reality of the Church is the "Body of Christ." We believe that God is a community: the Trinity is one God consisting of three Persons. We're made in God's image and likeness, so we're also made for community. God made Eve because "it is not good that the man should be alone; I will make him a helper as his partner" (Gen 2:18). When they were married, it was said that they became "one flesh" (Gen 2:24). The body is how we experience everything because we are corporal. God also told us that our bodies are a "temple of the Holy Spirit" (1 Cor 6:19). Bodies are important, and companioning together in them is important. Jesus sent the apostles out to preach the gospel two by two, and told us, "For where two or three are gathered in my name, I am there among them" (Matt 18:20). Jesus gathered people around him in groups as apprentices and continuously stressed the importance of community by restoring those he healed to them. He also gave us his body in the Eucharist, which we also call the Body of Christ.

Saint Paul refers to the Church as the Body of Christ throughout his letters. He says, "For just as the body is one and has many members, and all the members of the body, though many, are one body, so it is with Christ. For in the one Spirit we were all baptized into one body—Jews or Greeks, slaves or free—and we were all made to drink of one Spirit" (1 Cor 12:12-13). This means that, while we're all unique individual members, we're joined together by the love of God to complete the mission of Christ by working together. If one of the members has a victory, we all do, and if one has trouble or sickness, we all do. We can't function without any of the members missing, even the ones that we consider to have less honor. We also need each other for the special gifts that we each offer—each one is necessary for the fulfillment of our destinies, and the destiny of the world. This is what Church is about—learning to appreciate the giftedness of each member, helping them to reach their potential, and growing in our knowledge and love of God through intimacy with our community. Because we are so unique, and have unique circumstances, there are myriad ways that the Body of Christ might live this out.

The City: A Lovely Bunch of Coconuts

The City was an awful place when The Tick was assigned there. It was overwhelmed by crime, and the criminals were overrunning it pretty much unchecked. The City wasn't at a loss for heroes—it had them on every corner, rooftop, and at every diner counter—it was crawling with heroes. But the heroes who were supposed to be defending The City were disorganized, confused, and at odds with one another, causing one another to fail. They were disenchanted and most of them were, at best, mentally unstable. Things would get very ugly if Die Fledermaus and American Maid (spoofs of Batman and Wonder Woman) showed up at the same time. They had dated, and you know what happens when ex-boyfriends and -girlfriends get together.

It took the presence of one even more unstable than the rest to get them inspired, somewhat organized, and working together (although, that took time). The Tick was a total and complete nut. He was "nigh invincible," so he had *that* going for him, and he was braver than brave—the kind of brave that only comes in one flavor: insanity. You couldn't pack any more enthusiasm into his six-foot, six-inch frame if you tried. He was daunted by nothing, and saw everything as an opportunity to do justice. And he was *invested*. The second that he was assigned to The City at the Superhero Convention, he was *all in*. He wasn't very smart; he just kind of plowed through villains instead of using any strategy. He was exactly what the superheroes of The City needed to get them going. He wasn't any smarter or saner than the rest of them, but he was *effective*. The others saw that something could be done, and so they followed his lead.

The Tick's sidekick, Arthur, had been an accountant but came across a moth suit that enabled him to fly. He felt that this suit was an invitation to embrace his destiny—that he was to be something more, but he didn't know what. He started wearing it in public and was fired. It didn't help that the moth suit really looked like a bunny suit, and he was out of shape, so he looked ridiculous, besides looking out of place.

The day he was fired was the day that Arthur met The Tick. The Tick was immediately drawn to Arthur because he recognized that they had the same mission—not because of anything in Arthur's attitude or his courage or even anything he said; he was just dressed properly for adventure. Arthur was hesitant; in fact, downright reluctant, to get involved in superhero activities too quickly. There was nothing heroic in Arthur except for a slight inkling...something that could be developed...but wasn't quite right in front of him. He was brought along with The Tick almost kicking and screaming—definitely screaming—when they went up against the Idea Men in their first adventure together. Arthur was terrified. But he was also smart, and that made up a bit for The Tick's lack of caution or planning. They defeated the Idea Men and saved The City. Arthur still wasn't convinced that this was the life for him, but he kept hanging around The Tick (well, The Tick wouldn't leave Arthur's couch—Arthur actually couldn't get rid of him), and this changed his life.

Like The City, the Church is full of really, very good people... and also horrendously mean people...and unbelievably crazy people. Oh, we're full of *all kinds* of people. Some in the Church want to do things the way we always have done them because we have always done them this way. Others want to scrap everything and start fresh, copying what the Church of What's Happening Now is doing. And then, there are some who just think whatever pops into their heads is what we should be doing.

The life of the Church is supposed to take root in and affect every aspect of our lives. It's not just education; it's not just worship; it's not just charity; it's not just family life, not just women, not just men, not just kids, not just divorced and separated. It's everything and everyone. So, it takes all kinds of personalities and people with all kinds of experience to minister to everyone who comes to us. Some of the best ministries that I know of came as the result of angry, or crazy, or timid, or ultra-kind, or conservative, or liberal, or not-sure-where-they-fit-in people looking for *something*. Some of the most impressive and moving moments that have happened in our church happened because of something someone who would be considered "fringe" did or said. Everyone is necessary. Everyone is welcome. Everyone has a place.

The City reminds me of a few aspects of Church. The Heroes of The City were good, well-meaning people who were floating without a compass. Instead of being guided, considerate, effective team players, they were drifting into each other's way and causing chaos. As members of society and of a church, we can't work that way, either. If we do, we risk more than just being ineffective—we risk turning good people away from where God has called them to serve. If we are not seeing the big picture, but are each trying to rule our little fiefdom, or if we are envisioning ourselves as the only important member and nourishing bitterness for one another, then we aren't accomplishing anything but chaos. And that's the opposite of what God is about. We need to see one another, to serve one another, and to allow ourselves to be served in our need. One of my professors in grad school used to tell us to say three times a day, "I am not the Messiah." Because I'm not. And neither are you. We're members of one Body; which, if it's not working together, will fall together.

Like Arthur, we have something inside our hearts but don't necessarily know how to classify it, or how to grow it. We don't need to be a huge personality who's doing something completely different than what's been done before. We don't need to be the smartest or most talented person in the world. We don't need to be entirely sane—in fact, it helps to be a little goofy to work in the Church. Sometimes, it's enough to just be willing to step out in faith and show up because something that is whispering in our hearts calls us to be greater.

This is something we can learn from The Tick. He was so unfettered by anything like reason that he never questioned what he should be doing. He knew clear as day what was evil and what wasn't. He had perfect trust in his calling to protect The City. His undaunted confidence in his vocation made him effective. I'm not suggesting that anyone should throw reason to the wind, but we could take a page out of The Tick's playbook. Make it the "I trust in my calling" page. We are all called—that should never be a question for us. We should be so trusting that God is going to bring to completion whatever God calls us to that we should see ourselves, in some ways, as being nigh invulnerable. Like The Tick, we all have massive amounts of talent. It could be a very specific talent, like having super strength, or it could be having a nice singing voice or being good at saying "Good morning" to people as they enter church. We don't have to be able to do everything. We need to be authentic, invested, and enthusiastic. We need to do what we're good at doing.

The City reminds me of small groups who come together periodically for a specific project or outreach—maybe a Bible study, faith-sharing group, or Pre-Cana team. It also makes me think of ecumenical or interfaith groups who come together not necessarily to form a new "church" but to foster elements of faith that enable them to be more aware and service oriented in the wider community. They might fight crime together, seek justice together, and further respectful dialogue that improves the well-being of the town or city that they all call home.

The Justice League: A Community in Tension

The early Church experienced some growing pains. It took the Church a while to figure out exactly what they needed to be doing, who they were, and what they should teach. They had to revisit what they had taken for granted as being the right way to live the law of God as the message of the gospel began to make its way to people who weren't Jewish. The apostles struggled, argued, and sometimes had to go their separate ways because they didn't agree with one another. The early bishops, at their councils, had to be locked in together for months at a time to come to a common understanding of theological concepts. It wasn't always civil; Santa Claus (Saint Nicholas of Myra) punched Arius in the face when he dared to speak his heretical ideas on Christology.

Even now, there are Christians who identify themselves as "conservative" or "liberal," or who others identify that way. There are some who would prefer that the Church get as close as it could be to the early Christian Church. There are others who would rather we get to just before Vatican II and stay there. Pope Francis wants a "poor Church for the poor," and some bishops and laypeople think that he's a bleeding-heart hippie. The point is that there is plenty of tension within the Church, and that's a good thing. We need a certain tension to keep us evaluating, clarifying, and becoming more honest. We are a big Church, and there's room for lots of different views, styles, and interpretations of how we should live the mission of Christ.

This is what the members of the Justice League do for each other; they bring varying perspectives and backgrounds that simultaneously enrich and challenge the group. When speaking of the Justice League, a distinction must be made immediately—which Justice League? Members come and go, and so it could be any number of combinations of heroes that we are discussing. We will stick to Batman, Superman, Wonder Woman, Green Lantern,

Flash, Hawk Girl, and J'onn J'onzz (Martian Manhunter). In the animated movie *The Justice League*, released in 2002, J'onn J'onzz comes to Earth to try and warn the inhabitants of an impending attack by invaders that destroyed all life on Mars, except for himself. As he got to Earth, he was intercepted and held prisoner, having the only sample of a plant that can immobilize the invaders destroyed in the process. Because he's psychic, J'onn J'onzz can contact the heroes of Earth telekinetically and summon them to come together. None of them knows why they were called, or by whom, but they come.

Right from the beginning, there's tension among the group. Batman doesn't fully trust anyone and prefers to work alone. He only calls Superman for help when there's no other choice. Superman is friendly, collaborative, and willing to do whatever is best for everyone. He's a real team player. Wonder Woman is new on the scene; there's some doubt about her ability and her origin (maybe because she's a she?). Of course, she proves herself to be brave, independent, and capable immediately. Flash always thinks he's the best at everything and tends to take things too lightly, and Green Lantern is used to cooperating at an extremely high level; he's not fond of being held back by the inexperience of others. He's all about efficiency and business. Hawk Girl is big on offense, and courageously strikes first in battle.

As they go into battle together, they begin to build trust, camaraderie, and sincere care for one another. They aren't just risking their lives to protect their own interests, but to protect their friends-at-arms, and it's clear that they all feel that the larger goal is more important than their own lives.

Seeing humankind behaving badly when they believe that they're going to be conquered and destroyed, a conversation between Wonder Woman and J'onn J'onzz occurs in which Wonder Woman wonders whether humanity is worth all the fuss. J'onn J'onzz says that he's been exactly where the earthlings are now. He encourages her not to judge them too harshly; he's felt the fear that grips them and is therefore empathetic. After seeing the good that humans can do, Wonder Woman eventually comes to find the will of humanity "intriguing."

Once the enemy is defeated, the question of "what if it happens again" is raised. Batman, being the fixer that he is, comes up with an immediate plan. He builds a space station to monitor any threats that might make their way near Earth in the future. He invites the other heroes aboard, and they decide that they are better together than apart, and form the Justice League— everyone but Batman, that is. He'll set it all up, but he's not what you would call a "joiner." He's the guy who is happy to share his skills when there's a specific need, but isn't really interested in being part of the large group on a regular basis. J'onn Jonzz muses over his being the last of his race, sadly, but Superman is in the same spot. Superman appeals to him to make Earth his home as Superman did, and the Justice League his new family. It's a perfect fit.

Driven by a common mission, common values, and common experiences, the Justice League becomes a home for these heroes. A couple have left their homes to be a part of this thing that they believe in, others lost their homes, and still others are from Earth but don't really fit in. The League is the home where they can know and be known, where they can be supported in their sense of mission and destiny. They are all together because they realized that they're more effective as a unit than they would be as individuals, even though they're high-functioning individuals who are used to being the expert in their fields. Their opinions will differ, and with each challenge they face together, they will find challenges to themselves and to the group.

In 1 Corinthians, Paul exhorts the budding Church, "Now I appeal to you, brothers and sisters, by the name of our Lord Jesus Christ, that all of you be in agreement and that there be no divisions among you, but that you be united in the same mind and the same purpose" (1 Cor 1:10). He had to say this because they weren't. They were in the "same mind and purpose" in that they all were doing their best to live the call they had received in their baptism. They were trying to learn whatever they could about Jesus and the scripture. But there was also a rivalry among them; and they weren't the only community to experience this. The Christians in Rome were divided; the Jewish converts thought that they were better because they knew the Law of Moses. The pagan converts thought that they were better because they weren't burdened with all that stuff and could begin their relationship with God fresh.

As it says in Ecclesiastes, "There is nothing new under the sun" (Eccl 1:9). We can all identify with it because we've all been there. Whether at work, on a sports team, or in some organization, the members are bound by a common purpose, but that doesn't mean they see themselves as equals or have the same preferred procedures to accomplish the goal. That kind of tension can be a source of trouble for a church, or, if managed properly, can be a source of life. Being of "one mind," like Paul talks about, doesn't mean they're robots. It means that everyone is heard and respected, which creates a safe place for constructive conflict to occur.

The members of the Justice League are seriously effective because they each have something distinct to offer and because they allow each member to do what they do best. They're effective because they trust one another and know that each has the highest good as their priority. The Church thrives on challenge. Our communities should naturally bring comfort and support in our lives and efforts, but the temptation for too much comfort must be resisted, because too much comfort can lead to stagnancy. We live in a big Church, and there is so much room for variety and diversity. If we honor that, like the Justice League, our gifts can be used to their fullest, making us truly effective.

The Avengers: A Planned Community

Both the heroes of The City and the Justice League grew from a sort of grassroots, organic process. The Avengers were "assembled," and not by their own choosing. They were a very different bunch of people with special gifts that the government saw as a weapon against extraterrestrial evils. They didn't necessarily like each other at first, and weren't keen on giving up their autonomy—to the government or to the team. While community can certainly be intentional, it can't be forced; and this diverse community had to struggle to find their way.

Bruce Banner was a scientist who was accidentally exposed to a massive dose of gamma rays that altered his cellular structure, causing him to change into a "hulk" in times of stress or anger; a creature that was crazy powerful and not entirely within Bruce's control. Not feeling especially safe to be around, Bruce resisted the idea of having to come when called. He is a kind and gentle man by nature, and was terrified of hurting the innocent when in his hulk state.

Following in his father's footsteps, Tony Stark was also something of a scientist; he was a brilliant inventor, mostly of weapons and defense systems, including his Iron Man suits in their various incarnations. He's used to functioning on a high level *alone*. He chooses his collaborations, and they are only as deep as he needs them to be to fit his purposes, which are almost entirely business. Neither Bruce nor Tony was keen on being told what to do by any authority figures. Both Bruce and Tony wanted to make the world a better place through their scientific efforts, but there's a sharp contrast between their methods of choice. They probably wouldn't have chosen each other's company out in the world, but had to find a way to coexist in their planned crime-fighting community.

Captain America is all about the team. Having been a small, scrawny weakling who wanted nothing more than to defend the weak and fight the Nazis, he willingly allows himself to be augmented so that he can be as strong in body as he is in heart. Through more science, he is made enormously buff and given a shield to aid him in his battles. Unlike his soon-to-be friends, he *wants* to belong to a team—the U.S. Army and then the Avengers. He just wants to serve in whatever capacity will be most useful to the weak and helpless.

Thor is used to working on a team back in Asgard, and he has led people in battle. He enjoys working with a trusted group of friends, and fights at his best in that situation. He is somewhat torn between two worlds but has both affection for, and a personal commitment to, humanity. Between his love for Jane Foster and his feeling responsible for the trouble his brother,

Loki, caused, Thor developed an appreciation for Earth and its inhabitants.

Like many of the other hero group franchises, the Avengers change members periodically. Ant Man, Wasp, Black Widow, and Hawkeye are used to being involved in covert missions in which they need to rely on others, but still somewhat acting alone. They are all self-reliant in situations that include a distant support team.

Planning and strategy only go so far when you're talking about community—that common sense of mission, accomplishment, and personal freedom while working within the group is crucial. Even the serious team players in this group, Captain America and Thor, struggle with what is asked of them sometimes, and have difficulty working within the requirements of S.H.I.E.L.D. In *Captain America: Civil War*, the Avengers become so regulated that they become divided and even split up. Incidents like this occurred in the early Church with small events like Paul and Barnabas going their separate ways, and it also occurred in our more recent history with what must be the biggest tragedy in the Church—the development of numerous Christian denominations. I have profound respect for my Protestant brothers and sisters, and I believe that our communities have much to teach and learn from one another, but the fact that we seek to live the mission of Christ and aren't united in that mission is devastating.

Jesus established the Christian community. He put Peter in charge and told the apostles what their job was, too. He made it clear that there was to be a structure governing the community and that authority would be placed with them. He said, "And I tell you, you are Peter, and on this rock I will build my church, and the gates of Hades will not prevail against it" (Matt 16:18). That's great news, because we can rely on the fact that God gave us a human authority that we can look to, and God promised that no matter how badly we get off track, we will always have God's help. Because, let's face it, the gates of Hades can only get near the Church if we invite that trouble in...kind of like the Tesseract that S.H.I.E.L.D. tried to make into a weapon, but Loki used as a transport to Earth with the intention of bringing the Chitauri through to invade. S.H.I.E.L.D. invited a hellish trouble by using evil to try and fight evil. Lucky for the world, the Avengers were there to beat Loki and the Chitauri back from whence they came.

The apostles had the benefit of apprenticing with Jesus for three years before they were on their own, and the Holy Spirit was their guide, counselor, and helper, but that didn't mean that developing the community was going to be easy. Within a very short time of having received the Holy Spirit and their mission in full, they had to adjust what they were doing and expand the authority structure to accommodate their growth. In Acts of the Apostles, we're told that while the apostles were trying to teach and take care of the poor, some in the community were being overlooked and their needs not fully met. The apostles knew that their first priority had to be teaching, so they "called together the whole community of disciples," saying, "Therefore, friends, select from among yourselves seven men of good standing, full of the Spirit and of wisdom, whom we may appoint to this task, while we, for our part, will devote ourselves to prayer and to serving the word" (Acts 6:2–4). These deacons would live the vocation of *diakonia*, which is service. They came to know the needs of the community and developed a liturgical role through their service. It was they who would bring the needs of the community to prayer, and to collect and bring the bread to share. They preached the gospel through their service, and eventually that translated to their proclaiming the gospel at Mass.

As the gospel made its way to pagan territories, it became clear that further adaptations were going to be necessary in the way the community lived God's Law. This is one of the cases in which diversity expanded Christian thought and practice in wonderful ways. Circumcision was a fine practice if you were Jewish—it would happen in infancy. When you get to adult pagan men, it's a totally different story. It was something of a deterrent, as one may imagine, to prospective converts. The holiness code regarding food was another barrier. In the first twenty or so years of the establishment of the community after Jesus's death, it became necessary that a council of the bishops (the apostles) occur.

The council of Jerusalem tackled some very touchy and serious issues. It changed things about the practice of faith that were deeply ingrained for the good Jewish men and women who walked with their Jewish teacher. There was disagreement, dissension, and truly challenging dialogue. And they were open to change; they allowed the Spirit to direct them, and, though it was rough, the community grew through the discomfort. Some people, who weren't on board and wanted to hold back the progress, were causing trouble in the churches. The apostles sent a message to the Gentiles, saying, "Since we have heard that certain persons who have gone out from us, though with no instructions from us, have said things to disturb you and have unsettled your minds, we have decided unanimously to choose representatives and send them to you, along with our beloved

Barnabas and Paul" (Acts 15:24–25). And there was much rejoicing.

Flexibility without giving up the foundation of our faith was key in the beginning and is key now. Too much rigidity, too much confidence in our correctness to the point of being deaf to the need to evolve isn't healthy. When Luther called for reform in the Church, he was right about a lot of it. We've changed a good deal of the things he identified as problems within the Church. He wasn't right about everything, though, and if he had been open to waiting a little longer, and if the Church authorities had been more open to admitting where we have invited the gates of Hades in, our history could have been very different. We might not be a scandal to the world that speaks of division, where instead Paul says that we should, "be of the same mind, having the same love, being in full accord and of one mind" (Phil 2:2). We're weaker apart. Division is the tool of the evil one— "And if a house is divided against itself, that house will not be able to stand" (Mark 3:25).

Looking back to *Captain America: Civil War*, we see how an overly controlling structure causes division among our heroes, who had, against all odds, become a team built on trust and common mission. It came to be that the United Nations wanted to have the authority over the Avengers to give them assignments and restrict them from engaging threats that the heroes had identified but that the United Nations felt weren't worth it. They were also fearful of what harm the Avengers might do on their own; they *had* already caused large-scale collateral damage in one of their missions, and innocent people were killed.

It wasn't only the United Nations who was afraid; some of the citizens of the world were afraid and some of the heroes, having been the ones who caused harm to innocent people in their attempt to neutralize the villains, were also afraid. They were filled with self-doubt and confusion, which made them want to give up the responsibility of choosing in which frays they would become involved.

It became a question of freedom for the two factions within the Avengers—some felt convicted that they should have the freedom to not be directed by the state, which could lead to horrendous corruption, and some wanted freedom from having to decide their future. Their new situation presented a real difficulty; if they abdicated their culpability by becoming a politically run special ops, they risked being manipulated; if they refused to become monitored by the state, they became renegades and outlaws. Both options left them in an unsettling place. Amazingly, the ones who would be more likely to be fine with operating outside the law were the ones who wanted to stay within it, and the ones who were all about trusting in authority now found themselves contradicting it.

Jesus said, "No one can serve two masters; for a slave will either hate the one and love the other, or be devoted to the one and despise the other" (Matt 6:24). The Church in the Middle Ages had a religious and political conflict. Once Christianity was no longer illegal and even became the state religion throughout a good deal of Europe, things got complicated for the Church. Princes were bishops and parishioners were subjects. People who weren't called to ministry used it, rather, as a social climbing tool; and they didn't care who they stepped on to get higher. If you can believe it, the power even went to some authorities' heads. The temptation to abuse power was too much for many men, and the mission of the hierarchy was certainly compromised. Because the leadership was so concerned with keeping their ill-gotten power, fear motivated them a good deal. Separation of church and state is crucial for the mission of the Church to progress authentically.

When the United Nations wanted the Avengers under their thumb, they faced a similar concern. Among both Avenger camps the heroes wanted the same thing—to fight evil and bring justice and safety to those who couldn't gain it for themselves. They wanted to fight side by side to defend the world from any threat that would come their way. But fear had a foothold within the Avengers and within the world community. And, as Yoda says in *The Empire Strikes Back* (yes, I did just switch franchises mid-thought, but it's apropos), "Fear leads to anger. Anger leads to hate. Hate to suffering." Whether there's division among the Avengers or the Church, fear leads to a dilution of mission, which thwarts our efforts to bring justice, which brings suffering to ourselves and to the world.

The X-Men: Mutants for a Better World

If ever there was a model for what Church should be, it's the X-Men. Charles Xavier, in his abundant compassion and care, set up a safe place for people who were at odds with the culture—again due to the fear of others—to learn how to become their best selves in the service of the world. What's most beautiful about Professor X's leadership is the freedom which he instills in the mutants whom he's helping to shape. He offers the opportunity to every mutant to learn how to embrace, control, and use their powers. He gently encourages and invites each one to step out in faith as they adjust to who and what they are, himself believing that they will be accepted and loved by their families, and eventually trusted by the world.

Professor X is solid in what he believes is true and right, what is the proper way to live fulfilled in an uncertain world, and he's not shy about teaching it. He has a school for the "gifted," where he holds classes in all areas of study, which include living with their powers. Mutants are free to find their place in the world with his guidance, but not under his thumb. They make mistakes, as all people do; they lose hope and focus, but they don't lose their welcome at the school. Many of the mutants in his care come and go—Wolverine is periodically noncommittal; Mystique sometimes finds herself on the wrong side of things; many of the mutants fall away and come back. He never stops hoping that even the ones who have separated from his group and are committing villainous acts against humanity, especially his dear friend Magneto, will one day return. And, when any *do* return, it's without judgement and with open arms.

This is how God responds to us, and how the Church is called to respond to the people of God in every phase of their lives. Let's look at King David, the greatest king of Israel. Most people remember him for his bravery as a youth, slaying Goliath in one try with his slingshot. Or, you might remember him for the debacle with Bathsheba. And, by debacle, I mean rape. David, like most kings of the time, had a boatload of wives. But he was never content with what he had. He saw Bathsheba bathing on a rooftop and decided that he needed her for his collection. Well, it's good to be the king, and he got what he wanted. The only problem was that she was married to one of his generals...that, and now she was pregnant. So, David tried to cover up his crime by making sure Uriah, the husband, came home for a conjugal visit. That backfired because Uriah was so dedicated to his service of the king, the ark of the covenant, and his men, he refused to enjoy his home life as long as the mission was not accomplished. Uriah's honor in the face of David's sin got him killed. David had him betrayed by his troops in battle; they stepped back and left him in the front line all by himself to be slaughtered by their enemy.

Enter Nathan, prophet of God. Nathan knows the truth and comes to David for what we would call today a "come to Jesus" talk. Knowing how headstrong he is, Nathan had to approach the correction in a roundabout way. Nathan told David a story, asking for his opinion of the main character. The wealthy man had a lot of sheep. His neighbor, who was poor, had only one. The rich man was having company, so he took the poor man's sheep and made a feast of it for his guests. Nathan asked if this was just, and what should happen to the man. David was outraged at the greed that this man displayed and replied, "As the LORD lives, the man who has done this deserves to die; he shall restore the lamb fourfold, because he did this thing, and because he had no pity" (2 Sam 12:5-6). Nathan said, "You are the man!" (2 Sam 12:7).

David immediately accepted what he had done. He was devastated by the evil he perpetrated and God forgave him. David had been chosen in his youth to be this great king, and the one from whose family line would come the Messiah. God saw something in him, knew the sins he would commit (they didn't end with Bathsheba and Uriah), and remained faithful to the promise that God would be with him, even though David broke his faith with God.

It is a reality that everyone, human or mutant, grows at their own pace, that God shapes and molds them according to God's plan—not our own. Although we sometimes try to make everyone fit into a specific timeframe of readiness in formation, a standard or benchmark for where they should "be" in their relationship with God based on what age or grade they are in, it's not up to us. David was called as a youth to the kinship of Israel, but had to grow into the role, even after he was king. You might have a Saint Aloysius, whose first words were the names of Jesus and Mary and whose thoughts from his earliest days were trained on God; or you might have a Saint Augustine, who took well into his adulthood to discover that he needed God. Once he did, he quickly cultivated a desire to conform his life to God's will. Of course, he had the prayers and example of his mother, Saint Monica, working in his favor, but he needed to follow his own path to get there. If we had written Augustine off in his twenties, we would have lost a doctor of the Church.

Our call is to meet people where they are, and to help them to know God better—wherever they are in relationship or understanding. I can say with absolute certainty that if, in my youth (or even today), I was judged by other people's level of spirituality or knowledge, I would never have gotten as far as I have. I have been blessed to have guides and directors who took me as I was and helped bring me a little farther. This is what Charles Xavier does so well, and what our hierarchy and our parishes should model themselves after.

Implications for the Body of Christ

There are all shapes, sizes, colors, cultures, gifts, and talents within the Church. Diversity is our strength when we cultivate the gifts it brings. There are lots of ways of being Church and living out the mission that Christ gave us. From large parish communities, to small faith-sharing communities, to the Extraordinary Form of the Mass, to ecumenical prayer services; the Church is a big, big place with room for everyone.

I believe that superheroes have a lot to teach us about how to be Church. Although they have their differences and conflicts, no one is better at recognizing their own giftedness and appreciating the giftedness in others. And nobody does all shapes, sizes, and colors better than superheroes. In the first movie of *The Avengers*, when Loki is blathering on about how easily he'll conquer the world with his allies, Tony Stark recounts to him the heroes that he's going to find himself up against. Tony knows that they'll be wildly outnumbered, but he still believes wholeheartedly that what they *do* have to offer is better than anything Loki can bring. "We have a hulk," he says with perfect confidence. He trusts in their talent and fidelity. He can do his job, he'll let them do theirs, and they'll work in concert and save the planet.

The same goes for the X-Men, the heroes in the City, the Justice League, any hero group. A bumpy start? Sure—that's to be expected. But when they take their time to develop a rhythm and trust, they're unbeatable. If churches could function with the same level of humility—each person recognizing their gifts and the gifts of others without jealousy or rivalry—we would be unbeatable, too.

Some parishes have too many Captain America's and not enough Wonder Twins. No one *wants* to be the Wonder Twins. They're not "cool." But if you can turn into any animal or a bucket of water, but have no mighty shield, at some point you're going to have to face facts about the gift you *do* have. Instead of discerning the gifts they have and putting them at the service of the community, people sometimes get focused on what they *want* their gift to be. Conversely, the Church needs leaders who are willing to help people do that work, and to be strong and compassionate enough to be honest with people when they are not offering what they're best at. We've all listened to lectors who are poor at public speaking and choir members and cantors who shouldn't even sing in the shower. It's painful to think of the embarrassment they would feel if they found out in a cruel fashion that they aren't any good. It's up to the leadership to preserve those folks from putting themselves in that position to begin with.

Scripture tells us,

> To each is given the manifestation of the Spirit for the common good. To one is given through the Spirit the utterance of wisdom, and to another the utterance of knowledge according to the same Spirit, to another faith by the same Spirit, to another gifts of healing by the one Spirit, to another the working of miracles, to another prophecy, to another the discernment of spirits, to another various kinds of tongues, to another the interpretation of tongues. All these are activated by one and the same Spirit, who allots to each one individually just as the Spirit chooses. (1 Cor 12:7–11)

If everyone could speak in tongues, but there's no one to interpret, the gift of tongues is useless; Paul told us that, too. And if someone could *interpret* and withheld that from the community because they'd rather *speak* in tongues, they'd be doing everyone a terrible disservice.

Being the Body of Christ means that we're charged with the responsibility of bringing Christ's presence to every sector of human experience, being ambassadors and healers, peacemakers and teachers. Every Christian, by virtue of their baptism, is called to this in whatever way their particular abilities suggest. It's everybody's job to engage the culture, and to challenge it where it doesn't promote justice or safety for the most vulnerable people. It's everybody's job to raise the dignity of everyone we encounter.

Charles Xavier increased the dignity of both his pupils and enemies by seeing individuals for who they were. Try doing that when someone on your parish staff has been accused of unjust treatment or bias, or when your son is reprimanded unfairly by an elderly parishioner who forgot what babies are like, or when you visit a new parish and are told that you're "in my seat," or when you are invited to participate in a capital campaign and you already feel that the Church is "all about money." As a career pastoral staffer, I can tell you that some days, people you've never met will call or show up at the office and scream at you for an injustice that they perceive they have (and very well may rightly have) suffered at someone else's hand. The initial shock and hurt can make it hard to see the person in front of you at all. Yet, this is what Jesus challenges us to. We are required to listen closer, look closer, feel with, and understand the assumptions and flaws of the person who just got in your face without making it about you. Heroes do that with their enemies. Jesus told us to "love your enemies and pray for those who persecute you" (Matt 5:44). Sometimes the people in the pews present as enemies; it's up to us to try and make them into teammates.

Being the Body of Christ means, too, that each parish must serve the poor, the stranger, the sick—the suffering of any kind. Pope Francis spoke of our becoming a "poor Church for the poor." Paul said that he had "become all things to all people" (1 Cor 9:22). That doesn't mean that he's a social chameleon; it means that he made himself relatable to all people by allowing his shortcomings and weaknesses to serve the people he met.

Our world Church has a responsibility to teach with care and compassion the truth of the gospel, making sure that everyone sees God as God truly is, through our actions and teachings. If you ask me, this has to begin with ecumenism. Just as the early Christians listened to the Holy Spirit, allowing it to move and shape them into something new, we need to find ways to come together and allow God's unifying presence to work in us. If the way we present ourselves to the world doesn't express forgiveness, reconciliation, inclusion, and unity; if we can't figure out how to live as the Body of Christ, what hope do we have of expressing it to those outside our churches?

And, as parishes, it's crucial that every person finds a place; finds welcome and an authentic relationship with God. If we welcome everybody, then everybody will see themselves reflected in our communities and find support and help from people just like them. This should be reflected in our worship, our administration, our parish staff and volunteers, and in our pews and parking lots.

CHAPTER TWO

SUPERMAN AND ARAGORN

They're So Jesus

Dual Nature

Whenever we talk about God, our language immediately falls short of reality. Human experience and language fail to express the enormity of God, yet its important for us to try. There's no analogy, no word to fully capture what Jesus is, and while the characters of Superman and Aragorn are not a perfect representation of Jesus, they do capture elements of him that could be useful in exploring the person of Jesus.

One of the first things I learned about Jesus was that he has a dual nature; he's 100 percent God, 100 percent human—and yet he is one person. Now, I was never any good at math, but I know when something adds up to 200 percent. And while ridiculous numbers like that seem to be perfectly acceptable in today's math classrooms, when I was a child, there was no such thing as more than 100 percent. So, besides the math quandary of yesteryear, understanding how someone could be all-divine and all-human was a complete mystery to me. But as the nuns said, that's perfectly fine, because faith means a certain amount of mystery, and Jesus is that certain amount. Mystery in the

Catholic Church isn't something to be solved—you can't follow the clues and find the answer to the riddle—because it's not a riddle. Mystery in the Catholic sense is a truth that's simply too big for a puny human brain to comprehend...yet.

When we get to heaven and are in the state God ultimately intended for us, we'll be ready to experience the fullness of God without our heads exploding. But what to do until then? God gave us intellect and will so that we could understand God more deeply. The more we learn about the created universe, the more we'll understand the mind of God. Unfortunately, that doesn't help with our comprehension of Christ's dual nature here and now. As far as I'm concerned, the best place to look, for now, is in hero stories...right after a little philosophical diversion.

In philosophy, we learned Plato's theory of form and copy. Horrifically oversimplified, the form is the original—the reality—while the copy is a physical representation of that reality that we can experience firsthand and grasp well enough to discuss intelligently. For our purposes here, God is the form, and every superhero is the copy. Everything exists in God and exists fully with God: heroism, honor, truth, beauty, power—any attribute you can find in humanity or the inventions of human authors. The superhero comes close—but is never as good as God.

For me, Jesus is the prototype, and heroes reflect the way we would like to experience him in our reality, but can't, so we make stories that illustrate our hopes and dreams. While there are thousands of Christ figures in literature and other media, there are two heroes that express to me most perfectly Jesus's divinity and humanity: Superman and Aragorn, respectively. In the tradition of my favorite gospel Evangelist, John, let's start from the top down and talk about Superman first.

Son of Krypton

He was not of our world. His father destined him to come to Earth, where his powers would be far beyond those of all the natural inhabitants he would encounter. But he was sent as an infant: helpless and in need of care and protection before he would become the man he needed to be to fulfill his destiny. He was adopted by simple, good, loving people who hid his unusual beginning on this planet, bringing him up with a knowledge of God and a sense that he would be instrumental in making his adopted world a better, safer place for all people, especially the weak and marginalized—those who couldn't take care of themselves.

His father out in the stars knew that, with the powers and character he possessed, he would become what he was meant to be for this world. When he grew in experience and strength, he went off on his own to discover his destiny. He found a lonely place where he could test himself and discern his father's intentions for him. In his place of solitude, he found that he could speak with his father, who gave him insight into who he was and why he was here. His father gave him courage to live out the plan for him. Whenever he was unsure or discouraged, he would go to spend time with his father in a quiet place.

However, he never could spend a lot of time out there because every time he went to be alone, something would come up that required his attention: saving people from drowning, preventing creatures from other worlds from attacking people, or aiding someone in danger of death. Sometimes he himself was betrayed by the people he was trying to protect.

And then there's Jesus. His Father sent him here from outside of our world to save us by his supernatural power. He was sent here, small, weak, and vulnerable, born of a woman who was pure, faithful, and trusting. He was adopted by a marginalized man who was kind, generous, and loving. His parents brought him up to love God and care for the poor and needy. He was endowed with a sense of destiny and had to go away for a time to be alone with his Father so that he could be prepared for his mission. He would try and take time by himself to reconnect with his Father whenever possible, but he was always interrupted by the needs of others.

These humble circumstances hide enormous power that, when revealed, makes much of humanity nervous. In both the Superman story and high Christology, this power is the most important aspect of our heroes: the power to save humanity from every threat to their safety, while choosing to live in perfect humility. They both exemplify self-giving, self-emptying love for people whom they could easily destroy and who really don't appreciate the salvation they're repeatedly given.

When the movie *Superman* came out in 1978, Kal-El literally crashes into the lives of the older, barren couple, Martha and John Kent. His Kryptonian craft crash-lands only yards away from where they're driving, causing them to veer off the road and blow a tire. When they see the crater from the impact, John and Martha go to investigate. Martha sees a little boy standing there with his arms wide open to receive her and immediately falls in love with him. She acknowledges him as an answer to her prayers for a child, and he embraces her and returns that love instantly. John is hesitant—he wants to know the origin of the child. And that's perfectly responsible behavior...and very much like our pal Joseph, Jesus's adopted dad. As John is trying to fix the tire, the jack becomes dislodged and the truck falls. Kal-El lifts the truck's back end to help John complete his task. His new parents are flabbergasted by his strength. They realize that they've been given a very special charge. John concedes that the boy will bear his family name, making him Clark Kent, and begins to teach him about how to use his strength responsibly for the good of others. John dies when Clark is young, leaving him to care for his mother in her advanced years.

The Gospel of Matthew tells a very similar story, which we see exclusively from Joseph's viewpoint. He is asked to take charge of a son who doesn't belong to him, whose origin is explained but somewhat confusing, gives his name and legacy to the boy, and dies when he is young, leaving him to care for his mother in her advanced years.

Kal-El's appearance on Earth is remarkable. His power is remarkable, too. It's shown almost as soon as his new Earth family meets him. (Did I mention that *El* means "God" in Hebrew?) It's what will define him as an adult, what will cause comfort and relief among many, and fear and suspicion among others. Their fear is not wholly irrational—he could easily subjugate us to his will.

But Superman is *good*. He has no interest in personal gain. His intention is only to serve the world that took him in when he was an orphan. That kind of selfless giving is hard to understand, especially when it has all the power in the world behind it. How many of us, given the ability to walk up and take whatever we wanted with no one to resist us, wouldn't abuse this power? One of the most impressive things about his character is that it never seems to occur to him to abuse his power. He doesn't even want the accolades that come with the gratitude that people have for his protection.

He can fly, has what seems to be limitless strength, and defeats invaders from other planets, including villains from his own planet who were his father's mortal enemies; he even reverses an earthquake to save the woman he loves. And when he's fighting evil, his eye is always on the smallest, most helpless people who are caught in the crosshairs. He saves *everyone*.

The Gospel of John tells of Jesus's entrance to human experience in this way: "In the beginning was the Word, and the Word was with God, and the Word was God. He was in the beginning with God. All things came into being through him, and without him not one thing came into being. What has come into being in him was life, and the life was the light of all people. The light shines in the darkness, and the darkness did not overcome it" (John 1:1–5).

Jesus's entry into our world predates everything. Jesus was there when the Earth was created. Now, *that's* power! He has the authority to create, control, own, and require anything from anyone, and he shares perfect equality with the Father and the Holy Spirit. He is the Lord who doesn't lord it over anyone. In fact, Jesus's idea of a good use of authority is serving people who can't repay you.

In the Gospel of Matthew, Jesus says to the apostles, "You know that the rulers of the Gentiles lord it over them, and their great ones are tyrants over them. It will not be so among you; but whoever wishes to be great among you must be your servant, and whoever wishes to be first among you must be your slave; just as the Son of Man came not to be served but to serve, and to give his life a ransom for many" (Matt 20:25–28). This is paramount to understanding Jesus. He, like Superman, put himself entirely at the service of the world through what he felt was an appropriate use of his power.

Jesus's power is complete—unlike Superman, it doesn't require the energy from a yellow sun and can't be dampened by any kind of kryptonite. Yet Jesus hands himself over to humanity to do what they will with him, and what they will is to kill him. In chapter 3 of Genesis, we're told that God's intention for us was to live on this Earth in perfect joy and peace, but that we messed it up by being disobedient. Adam and Eve represent God's intention and our fallen nature. Death came into the world through our choice. And so, as a result of our sinfulness, we would die and we would require other things to die as a sacrifice to God for our forgiveness. Jesus came to repair that error— and he chose to be the sacrifice that would end our need for blood sacrifices. He was sinless but allowed us to hand him over when we were looking for blood.

When God saved Israel from the slavery of Egypt, God told the people to sacrifice an unblemished lamb and "take some of the blood and put it on the two doorposts and the lintel of the houses in which they eat it," and that, "The blood shall be a sign for you on the houses where you live: when I see the blood, I will pass over you, and no plague shall destroy you when I strike the land of Egypt" (Exod 12:7, 13). The Passover before Israel's salvation from slavery was a prefiguration of the world's salvation from the slavery of sin and death. Before he was arrested, Jesus anguished over his destiny. He knew what lay ahead and was not keen on it. But saving us was more important to him than his personal comfort and survival. We call Jesus the "Lamb of God" because he takes the place of animal sacrifice, and because his blood painted on the doorpost of our hearts makes the angel of death pass over us. Jesus made himself subject to his enemy— death—which was subject to him, so that death could no longer have any claim on us. The Father intervened and brought him back to us, saving us once and for all from the consequences of our ingratitude and sin.

With his vulnerabilities, Superman found himself in a similar situation in the movie *Man of Steel*. Zod and his crew had come to Earth for revenge against Superman's dad, Jor-El, for imprisoning them in the Phantom Zone, and demanded that the people of Earth hand him over or he and his nasty buddies would destroy Earth. Humanity was all for it—they turned on Superman, telling him to give himself up, saying that he wasn't even one of them. While he discerned with a local parish priest if handing himself over to his enemy was the right thing to do, he sat in a church in front of a stained-glass window that depicted Jesus at Gethsemane. He decided it was the right thing, and he did. His father helped him get out of that situation, and he was preserved so that he could continue to protect the ungrateful world that he had adopted.

Son of Númenor

Aragorn, son of Arathorn, son of Arvedui, son of Isildur, was the rightful king of the Dúnedain and all of the Men of the West. He was the one destined to unite the kingdoms of Middle-earth. His genealogy is important because he's the only one who has the right to claim the throne of the White City, Minas Tirith, the High City of Gondor. There was a time when the Men of the

West were united, but the temptation of the One Ring was too strong for one of them—Isildur, who, choosing not to destroy it, kept the Ring to become the most powerful ruler. That was utter foolishness because, for one thing, he already had sovereignty, and secondly, the Ring is pure evil, and can't be wielded by any mortal. Isildur was killed, the Ring lost, and the world of Men divided into factions.

While the Men of Gondor flourished, the Men of Númenor declined and dwindled. At the point of the story of Middle-earth when *The Lord of the Rings* takes place, the sons of Isildur had become very few, were secretive and set apart from the rest of the world, and appeared to be sinister wanderers, looked on with suspicion by the various peoples of the lands. Stories and prophecies about them were remembered and handed down, sometimes in songs, but were considered more like faerie tales than truths. They were known as the Rangers, remnants of the true heirs to the throne. In fact, they were quietly defending the borders and gathering intel about the growing strength of the Enemy—Sauron and his minions.

When Aragorn, the heir of Isildur, comes onto the scene as one of these Rangers, he's known as Strider, and people are generally afraid of him. He was sent by Gandalf to protect Frodo and his burden, the One Ring, so that he could be brought to a safe place where the fate of the Ring could be decided. Aragorn carries a weight with him—the weight of the failure of his ancestors—and the fear that he won't be any better. He's not ready to assume his proper position in the world when we first meet him, but he is made ready by having to face and embrace his destiny as savior of Middle-earth, accepting who he is and living it fully.

The Gospel of Matthew begins with a genealogy of Jesus for much the same reason. Matthew traces Jesus's pedigree all the way back to Abraham, and the first sentence of the Gospel is this: "An account of the genealogy of Jesus the Messiah, the son of David, the son of Abraham" (Matt 1:1). It's important for Matthew, who is Jewish and writing to Jewish Christians, that Jesus be linked to King David, the greatest king of Israel, the one from whom, according to the prophecy, the Messiah who would save the world would come. Throughout Scripture there are references to this prophecy, and there are very specific characteristics of the Messiah that are prophesied, too. It says in the Book of Isaiah that when the Messiah comes, "Then the eyes of the blind shall be opened, / and the ears of the deaf unstopped; / then the lame shall leap like a deer, / and the tongue of the speechless sing for joy" (Isa 35:5-6). It says, "He has sent me to bring good news to the oppressed, / to bind up the broken-hearted, / to proclaim liberty to the captives, / and release to the prisoners; / to proclaim the year of the LORD's favor, / and the day of vengeance of our God; / to comfort all who mourn" (Isa 61:1-2). In the time of the Messiah, "they shall build up the ancient ruins, / they shall raise up the former devastations; / they shall repair the ruined cities, / the devastations of many generations" (Isa 61:4).

In fact, this is what Jesus did. He shared news of God's mercy to the people who needed to hear it (which was everybody), brought comfort and healing to those who needed it, and undid the devastation of sin that had been steadily handed down from generation to generation. He rebuilt God's people into a new Church, bringing unity where there was division and a sense of mission where it had been lost to complacency.

When Jesus first came onto the scene in his public ministry, he had lived for thirty years as a fairly normal guy. He was so normal that when he started gaining a reputation for his teaching and healing and then went to his own hometown, people who knew him growing up wanted to know who he thought he was. They knew who he was—Joseph's boy. "They said, 'Where did this man get all this? What is this wisdom that has been given to him? What deeds of power are being done by his hands! Is not this the carpenter, the son of Mary and brother of James and Joses and Judas and Simon, and are not his sisters here with us?' And they took offense at him" (Mark 6:2–3). Why did he think he was so special? He lived the life of a day laborer just like his dad, took care of his mom, and apparently didn't do anything interesting enough to gain notice until after his baptism by John.

He was sort of like a Ranger—he was the True King of Israel, but remained incognito until it was time for him to act. And when he began his public ministry, there were still elements of mystery attached. He often healed people in private and asked them to keep it to themselves, offered little glimpses of what he really was to his apostles, taught and preached and cast out demons, and acted like it was nothing. He was humble and even hesitant to claim his throne, perhaps, in part, because his throne was a cross.

Over and over again, people and demons would call Jesus what he was—the Messiah, the Anointed, the One who would save Israel, the Son of God and Son of Man. But his response was steadily a variation of "My hour has not yet come" (John 2:4).

Aragorn was not hasty about becoming king, either. He waffled a lot about it, and delayed his claim until the very last minute possible. Even when he brought the unified armies to the

Gates of Mordor to buy Frodo some time to destroy the Ring in the fires of Mount Doom, and gave that awesome speech to rally the troops and give them courage, his true kingly nature was showing, but he wasn't yet interested in calling it what it was. That didn't matter so much, because the men were beginning to recognize his greatness and kingly bearing through his bravery and leadership. And, like Jesus, Aragorn had a lot of nicknames that belied his hidden, humble origins: Elfstone, Elessar, Man of the West, Isildur's Heir.

Aragorn was entitled to claim the authority over all the Men of the West. He also had claim over a somewhat different group of people: The Army of the Dead, or Oathbreakers in Dwimorberg. These folks had broken an oath to Isildur in battle hundreds of years before, and were doomed to live as ghosts until an heir of Isildur came along and gave them an opportunity to fulfill it and finally be put to rest. They turned the tide when they arrived at the Pelennor Fields and routed the Orcs and Easterlings. Then, released from their oath, they gratefully retired to eternal rest.

That part always reminded me of the Valley of the Dry Bones from Ezekiel:

> He brought me out by the spirit of the LORD and set me down in the middle of a valley; it was full of bones. He led me all around them; there were very many lying in the valley, and they were very dry....Then he said to me, "Prophesy to these bones, and say to them: O dry bones, hear the word of the LORD. Thus says the Lord GOD to these bones: I will cause breath to enter you, and you shall live. I will lay sinews on you, and will cause flesh to come upon you, and cover you with

skin, and put breath in you, and you shall live; and you shall know that I am the LORD." (Ezek 37:1–6)

Ezekiel goes on to say,

Mortal, these bones are the whole house of Israel. They say, "Our bones are dried up, and our hope is lost; we are cut off completely." Therefore prophesy, and say to them, Thus says the Lord GOD: I am going to open your graves, and bring you up from your graves, O my people; and I will bring you back to the land of Israel. And you shall know that I am the LORD, when I open your graves, and bring you up from your graves, O my people. I will put my spirit within you, and you shall live, and I will place you on your own soil; then you shall know that I, the LORD, have spoken and will act, says the LORD. (Ezek 37:11–14)

The dry bones people had broken the covenant with God; and their dryness is a sign of spiritual death. They can't be restored until the one who has authority over them gives them their life back and restores them to the covenant.

Christians believe that's exactly what Jesus did. Besides giving people their lives back by healing them and making them welcome again in their communities, giving spiritual life to the walking dead of the status quo in occupied Israel, and raising the literally dead to life again, we believe that Jesus went to the realm of the dead to preach the gospel in his dead time before he rose. The Apostle's Creed says that he, "descended into hell,"—to the dead—which is when he got around to that business. He presented himself to those who hadn't had the benefit of knowing him because they lived before he came in human form. He took whoever accepted what he had to say with him to heaven. He gave them eternal life.

When the final battle between the armies of Middle-earth and the evil alliance of Sauron was over, Aragorn entered the White City and went to the Houses of Healing. He was the only one who knew how to heal wounds inflicted by the Enemy. Éowyn, Shield Maiden of Rohan, and niece of King Théoden, had received a devastating wound when she killed the King of the Nazgûl—the Witch-king of Angmar—trying to save her uncle on the battlefield. She was in the Houses of Healing when Aragorn, who had entered the city to claim his throne, came in. He brought the correct herb to heal her and the others who had been wounded (including Faramir and Merry), causing a nurse to recall a song from her youth, "The hands of the king are the hands of a healer, and so shall the rightful king be known." One of the signs of his kingship, like that of Jesus, was that he would have the ability to heal on a level that no one else could.

Both Jesus and Aragorn were the rightful kings, both because of their ancestry and their worthiness. Both were unrecognized until the time was right for them to claim their authority, and both brought unity and peace that no other kings in their place had to offer. They were both prophesied, and both fulfilled the destiny of their forefathers.

Our Hero King

Let's return to where we started. Jesus's divinity and humanity both have significance for our experience of God through him. Catholics say that Jesus is the "fullness of revelation" and that there's nothing more we can learn about God that isn't included in the person of Jesus. Jesus is all-powerful and has every right and ability to force us to accept him as God Incarnate. But having that kind of power and authority also brings freedom. Because he can require our obedience, he doesn't need it. Everything already belongs to him. So, he leaves us to our own free will to accept him or not.

When God set the people of Israel apart and made a great nation of them, one of the conditions of the covenant was that God would be their King and they would follow whatever God asked of them. It worked for a little while, but after looking around at the other nations, Israel felt that they were missing out by not having a human king. They asked God for one and God told them that it was a bad idea. If they got a human king, they would get off track and things would get ugly. They persisted. Samuel even pulled the "Don't come crying to me!" thing that all parents say when their kid won't listen to reason: "And in that day you will cry out because of your king, whom you have chosen for yourselves; but the LORD will not answer you in that day" (1 Sam 8:18). They persisted. God allowed them to have one, and so they began with Saul. And, just as God said, things got ugly.

Jesus came to restore the proper order—like Aragorn, he came to be the one, true King that the people needed. The charges that were publicized on his cross acknowledged our unruliness; he was the True King, Jesus of Nazareth, King of the Jews, but it was meant as a mockery—mocking him for his apparent weakness and us for our blindness to God's presence.

As with Superman and Aragorn in various times, it looked like Jesus had lost. There was a scary moment or two when it looked like everything was going to hell in a handbasket and we'd never recover from it. The apostles were sure that it was over—they even hid, trying to preserve their own lives. But then there's that snippet from John: Jesus is a "light [that] shines in the darkness, and the darkness did not overcome it" (John 1:5). Jesus's divinity can't be wiped out or defeated; it predates and outlives evil. It has no equal. That's why whenever God or a representative of God shows up in Scripture, we're told, "Do not be afraid."

We also know that, since Jesus is truly human, and went through everything that any one of us could go through, he understands us perfectly. Jesus's power is so perfect that he put it away to be more like us; he even allowed himself the experience of needing to learn. The Gospel of Luke tells us that as a boy nearing manhood, "Jesus increased in wisdom and in years, and in divine and human favor" (Luke 2:52). Already perfect in knowledge, wisdom, and understanding, he subjected himself to learning these things from his parents, grandparents, rabbis, the Torah, and so on.

It was vital to our understanding of God's perfect love for us that Jesus experience everything that any other human would, including suffering. He could have prevented himself from feeling the pain of his scourging, crucifixion, and death, but instead suppressed his divinity to experience the whole thing. He wanted us to know that nothing stood between him and us—that nothing stands between God and us. He had the strength to be above it, but instead entered fully into it for our sake. "For we do not have a high priest who is unable to sympathize with our weaknesses, but we have one who in every respect has been tested as we are, yet without sin. Let us therefore approach the throne of grace with boldness, so that we may receive mercy and find grace to help in time of need" (Heb 4:15–16).

Jesus got angry and flipped tables, cried when his friends died, enjoyed good conversation with friends (and frenemies), felt pity for the sick and marginalized, laughed and danced at weddings, got frustrated and tried to get some alone time, knew that people only wanted him because he fed and healed them, was a refugee, lived in an occupied territory by an abusive regime, saw corruption, was rejected and mocked by the people who knew him growing up, felt the loss of his father, was betrayed and denied by his best friends, and handed his mother over to his friend while he looked at her, heartbroken, watching him die. That's a wide variety of human experiences. It's hard to wrap our brains around the bigness of Jesus's dual nature. It's a mystery deserving of our pondering, and it naturally engages our imaginations.

CHAPTER THREE

BATGIRL

The Church in Democratic Nations

Working with "the Man"

From the time Barbara Gordon was small, she wanted to be a crime-fighting superhero. She used to create characters and design their costumes, wishing that she would one day become one herself. Her parents were killed in a car accident, which led to her adoption by James and Barbara Gordon of Gotham City. She became infatuated with Batman, who was living her dream of the superhero life, and began to take steps to grab that dream herself. She convinced her adoptive father—the police commissioner—to enroll her in martial arts classes and learned what she could about fighting crime. When she was old enough, she tried for a career in law enforcement but was turned away for being too short. They didn't think she could do the job because of her height.

Barbara was brilliant: she earned a PhD, was the head of the Gotham Library, was awesome with technology, had a mind for detective work, and was disciplined in her physical abilities. Being the adopted daughter of a public figure, Commissioner Gordon, she knew what it meant to be on display, but she also could quietly watch her dad work and navigate tricky and dangerous situations. She observed his relationship with Batman and had a strong desire to fight crime in both of their worlds. She learned from her heroes to walk a thin line, keeping her public persona free from question for her dad's sake, and her superhero persona free from discovery for her own.

Barbara made a Batgirl costume before she had a reason to and had it with her at a fortuitous moment—Bruce Wayne and some other ultrarich guys had been kidnapped at a big soiree. Donning her new costume, she tried to rescue him but failed utterly. Bruce wound up having to rescue her. You can't win them all, and it was a valiant first try. She found her way into Batman's confidence and became part of the Bat "family." She lived two lives; one fighting ignorance, the other fighting crime, and each informed the other. They made her better at what she was doing, and made her more effective.

This is how I see the role of Catholic and Christian politicians. The thing that drives us, that informs our consciences and shapes our world view, is faith. Because of how deeply personal faith is, there's a component of it that is somewhat private—almost a secret identity that only God knows because only God can truly know anyone's heart. It's where our passion comes from, and where we are most perfectly authentic; where we're most perfectly ourselves. This is the Batgirl side in my analogy. Barbara's identity as Batgirl had to remain a secret, but her actions as Batgirl were decidedly public. This is another component of faith—if it's sincere, it must be personal, but not private. Faith is meant to be lived out in the public forum, and so by nature requires public activity.

When John F. Kennedy was running for president, there was concern that, as a Catholic, he'd be the pope's puppet. When he was questioned about it, his response was practical. He said, "I am not the Catholic candidate for President. I am the Democratic Party's candidate for President, who happens also to be a Catholic." His public identity had to be politician first, and it's not my place to comment on what kind of a Catholic he was. But there's no denying that his sense of social justice and quest for peace and scientific development would have been imprinted on him and nurtured by his Catholic upbringing. He wasn't a secret Catholic, but his public function had to have somewhat of a distance from his spiritual self.

It's gravely important to keep the separation of church and state—the country was concerned with this, and so was President Kennedy. That's a shared value between the founding fathers and our Church—a state religion is dangerous, but freedom of religion is imperative. Like Barbara and Batgirl, they each inform the other, but work in different ways to accomplish the same purpose.

The early Church made this distinction, and we continue to live by it. Some felt that in order for us to achieve true spiritual growth, we'd have to remove ourselves from the distractions of society. They thought that we couldn't live among sinners and remain pure. Others argued that Jesus didn't shy away from the world, but engaged it—especially sinners—and that was the mission that we were given. Jesus said that "those who are well have no need of a physician, but those who are sick; I have come to call not the righteous but sinners to repentance" (Luke 5:31–32). So, if we were just hanging out with people who thought and acted the way that we do (presuming that we're "healthy"), we're not carrying on Jesus's mission. And, while there is a place for monasticism, it's a specific vocation—it's not meant for everyone. Most people are called to live in the world and effect good for the general public.

Paul of Tarsus was a citizen of Rome and liked to claim that honor *a lot*. Especially when he was in trouble...which was *a lot*. He didn't try to distance himself from it, but used it as a vehicle for spreading the gospel. Saint Peter, as soon as he had received the Holy Spirit along with Jesus's other pals, went out and immediately addressed the crowd, "Men of Judea and all who live in Jerusalem, let this be known to you, and listen to what I say" (Acts 2:14). He was talking to everyone, people of "every nation under heaven" (Acts 2:5), because Jesus told the apostles to do just that: "Go therefore and make disciples of all nations, baptizing them in the name of the Father and of the Son and of the Holy Spirit" (Matt 28:19). You can't do that if you're not engaging the world.

Jesus also said that one of the ways we're supposed to spread the gospel, one of the ways we help people to encounter God, is by feeding the hungry, giving drink to the thirsty, clothing the naked, visiting the sick and imprisoned, and welcoming the stranger (see Matt 25:31–46). In fact, this isn't only *a* way to make God present to others, but *the* way we'll each be judged. You can't pass that test if you're not engaging the world.

All politicians in democratic societies have an amazing opportunity and obligation—to make sure that they're representing the citizens that they've promised to represent without prejudice or favoritism, and to uphold and protect the dignity of all people. They have the privilege of making laws that will set the tone for the country, and create standards for the treatment and care of the poor, vulnerable, and marginalized. Catholic and Christian politicians, while keeping church and state appropriately separate, can bring the values they were given by faith to life by effecting fair and compassionate laws that will make our country better and bring us closer to meeting the needs of all.

Like Batgirl, they walk a line between what they believe is just and right because their faith and reason tell them so, and what is reasonable and practical for the wider community. We need to be "the man," but we also must keep a healthy separation from "the man" to remember where our authority comes from and how we're expected to use it.

While You Were Sleeping

One of the difficulties in democratic societies is the balance of "self-interest" and our responsibility to countries that are less fortunate or in trouble with no way to defend themselves. American history has repeated itself several times in this aspect. We stayed, and continue to stay, out of conflicts where we saw the brutalization and decimation of peoples with horrifying cruelty. We ignored the destruction of borders, citizens, ethnic groups, and religions in World War II until we were attacked, despite other countries begging for help. We ignore the pleas of the helpless slaughtered by Boko Haram and ISIS, the cries of tiny countries under crushing debt that they can never repay. We help in marginal ways countries who suffer natural disasters, and ignore flammable tap water in mining towns with high cancer rates in our own country, and unprecedented earthquakes caused by our abuse of the Earth. Until it affects us personally, and affects the "right" people, we're apathetic and inactive.

Scripture warns of our becoming too comfortable, because comfort breeds drowsiness. National nap time. The prophets were concerned in great part with social justice and accused Israel repeatedly of their injustice toward the poor. The prophet Amos wrote, "Hear this word, you cows of Bashan who are on Mount Samaria, / who oppress the poor, who crush the needy, / who say to their husbands, 'Bring something to drink!' / The Lord GOD has sworn by his holiness: / The time is surely coming upon you, / when they shall take you away with hooks, / even the last of you with fishhooks" (Amos 4:1–2). Amos uses a formula of "for three transgressions and for four," listing the sins of the nations as he builds up to accusing Israel, God's people, of their sins. This means that their crime has been complete—three transgressions plus four equals seven, and seven is perfection. Each of the nation's sins are related to war, social justice issues, and their treatment of the poor.

John speaks for God in the Book of Revelation, saying, "I know your works; you are neither cold nor hot. I wish that you were either cold or hot. So, because you are lukewarm, and neither cold nor hot, I am about to spit you out of my mouth. For you say, 'I am rich, I have prospered, and I need nothing.' You do not realize that you are wretched, pitiable, poor, blind, and naked" (Rev 3:15–17).

But because God is God, it doesn't end there—neither of the stories do. God invites us to wake up. "Listen! I am standing at the door, knocking; if you hear my voice and open the door, I will come in to you and eat with you, and you with me. To the one who conquers I will give a place with me on my throne, just as I myself conquered and sat down with my Father on his throne. Let anyone who has an ear listen to what the Spirit is saying to the churches" (Rev 3:20–22).

This reminds me of one of the coolest parts of *The Two Towers* from *The Lord of the Rings*. King Théoden of Rohan had fallen under a spell woven by the great wizard turned evil, Saruman. Saruman had sent Gríma, called "Wormtongue," to keep Théoden under the spell, making him weak, ineffective, unaware of what was going on around him, and apathetic to the growing danger that threatened his people. Théoden never left his throne—somewhat of a mockery of his latent authority. He had abdicated his power, giving it over to someone else to make decisions or keep from making any decisions, which would lead to the destruction of his land. His niece and nephew tried to warn Théoden of the impending doom, but Gríma's whispers prevented him from seeing the truth.

Eventually, Gandalf, Aragorn, Legolas, and Gimli arrived in Rohan, where Gandalf brought Théoden back into reality. Events like this happen in Western culture frequently. In our current context, we are so bombarded with "news" spun so far from reality by pundits that it can be very, very difficult to find the truth. It's far too easy to settle into a version of reality that suits any individual's personal opinions just by choosing the news network that will support their sensibilities. Some will be lulled into inaction, believing their negative views about others to be justified, and the others to be unworthy of their help. Some will be paralyzed into inaction by the enormity of the world's problems, not knowing how they can make a difference.

In fact, Christians in democratic nations don't have the luxury of inaction. We've been given an immeasurable gift and responsibility to help shape and change the world—to discover the truth and to make it known, and to work tirelessly until the needs of the weakest and most vulnerable members of society are met. We have a voice through our vote, peaceful demonstrations, free speech, and a free press. If we aren't using the privilege of that voice to speak for those who can't be heard, we aren't living the gospel, and we're doing our country a disservice. We're meant to be good citizens, and in democracy, good citizens are those who participate in the political dialogue. We have the responsibility to elect representatives and officials who will uphold gospel values.

Lucky for us, Scripture is very clear about how to live justice. Repeatedly in the Hebrew Scriptures God gives the definition of *justice* as "caring for the widows, orphans, and aliens." "For the LORD your God is God of gods and Lord of lords, the great God, mighty and awesome, who is not partial and takes no bribe, who executes justice for the orphan and the widow, and who loves the strangers, providing them food and clothing. You shall also love the stranger, for you were strangers in the land of Egypt" (Deut 10:17–19). If our elected officials made this their baseline to measure their success, we'd be in great shape. In democratic nations, it's our job to hold them accountable on these points, and to make sure that our actions are in line with these values, too.

Looking back at *The Lord of the Rings*, Théoden wasn't the only one sleeping. The Hobbits liked to live in their little Shire bubble; they didn't want to know what was going on in the rest of Middle-earth. They weren't interested in having company from the wider world, and didn't look kindly on any Hobbits who got the mind to travel. They wanted to remain insulated so that they wouldn't be touched by the world's troubles. They found that you can only do that for so long—eventually the world's troubles will come to you.

The Ents had a similar worldview. They just lived their tree-people life, which was becoming increasingly isolated and apathetic. Treebeard, one of the Tree Herders, commented to Merry and Pippin when they sought refuge in Fangorn Forest that many of the trees were no longer speaking, and more and more were simply sleeping. It wasn't until the fight was brought to them that they paid attention to what was happening around them. Saruman was cutting down their forests—trees that Treebeard knew personally—and burning them to make weapons for their final assault.

The point is that if, like the Hobbits and Ents, we wait for the fight to come to us, we've waited too long. The poor and victims of violence are our concern. Jesus told us that we *are* our brother's keeper. He reiterated the Jewish teaching to "love your neighbor as yourself," reminding us that *everyone* is our neighbor. He even takes several steps further to warn us that those who are neglected here will surely find comfort in heaven, and those who have done the neglecting will suffer eternally.

In the story of the rich man and Lazarus in the Gospel of Luke (16:19–31), Jesus turns the tables entirely on the cultural norms of the time. People believed that if you were rich, it was because you were good and God was blessing you, and if you were poor, it was a punishment for being sinful—the same went for people who were ill, or had demons, or were victims of violence. That's a very convenient worldview, because it could easily give one the impression that they aren't responsible for those who are suffering. But even with that belief, it was expected of all Jews that they would care for the poor and try to ease the suffering of their countrymen. The rich man ignores this teaching and ignores the suffering at his doorstep.

Lazarus is a poor man who sat outside the rich man's gate begging. He was so destitute that he was covered in sores that dogs would come by and lick while he sat there helplessly. The rich man would literally have to step over him to get into his house, but chose to be blind to the man's plight daily. When they each died, Lazarus went to the bosom of Abraham while the rich man went to hell. Even then, the man told Abraham to have Lazarus bring him water. He was so entrenched in his entitlement that he couldn't even accept his new circumstances. Just as he refused to acknowledge Lazarus's suffering in life, he refused to see his place of honor in the afterlife.

Another interesting point here is that in the scriptures, only particular people are given names. We know Lazarus's name, but the other guy is just another guy—he's defined by his material wealth, and has lost his rightful identity in it. He's a nameless man of no importance because he threw away everything that mattered—including his own soul. The rich man was lulled into inaction by his desire for personal gain and lost everything in the process.

Although her crime fighting was a secret to most of the world, Barbara Gordon chose to define herself by putting her sense of justice into action. She risked much by donning her cowl: bodily harm, being discovered if anything ever went wrong, putting her dad in an awkward situation, and the risk that every hero takes, that of losing your true identity in the shadows of your public identity. With Batman as her mentor, she could retain a foot in both worlds, by day fighting ignorance through dispensing knowledge, and by night keeping the rogues of

Gotham in check. She didn't lose herself to either of her passions and was effective in both because her heart was centered on justice.

This is a concern for every individual, every family, every Christian community, and every democratic nation. We have the unique ability to choose how we'll be defined, and by what name we'll be called. We can remain sleepy and ignorant, accepting of half-truths, twisted-truths, spun-truths; or we can demand truth and accountability; first by living it, and next by voicing it publicly until it's represented and effected in our legislation. The prophet Hosea, in chapters 1 and 2, was told to name his children names that meant "not pitied" and "not my child" when they were born to a mother who was sleeping around (which represented us worshipping other gods). Later, after Hosea was told to go and woo her to come back, the kids' names were changed to "Children of the living God" (Hos 1:10). Just like it was up to Gomer, Hosea's wife, what her legacy would be, it's up to us what ours will be.

Live Every Day Like Dorothy Day

When Batgirl first entered the scene in *Batman: The Animated Series*, Bruce Wayne had gone undercover and he was out of commission for a bit. He was also investigating an incident that cast a shadow on Commissioner Gordon, which landed the commissioner in jail. Batman was working on proving his innocence, but Barbara didn't know that. She knew that her dad was in trouble, and Batman was nowhere to be found to help, so she took matters into her own hands. She grabbed her costume and headed for the streets. Being new at crime fighting, she had some trouble and almost got herself killed. Robin, who was also not idle while Batman was away, tried to stop her for her own protection—it was clear that she was a novice. He grabbed at her and caught the back of her cowl, freeing her hair. The revelation—"A girl?"—surprised him, but didn't cause him to dismiss her. Even if she wasn't a pro, she had some mad martial arts and acrobatic skills. And, because it was clear that they were on the same side, Robin joined in with Batgirl to try and stop the baddies.

It reminds me of Jesus saying, "Do not stop him; for whoever is not against you is for you" (Luke 9:50), when the disciples were upset that someone they didn't know was casting out demons using Jesus's name. When we're on the same side, when we're working toward the same goal, we need to put our differences aside and be a stronger force together.

Until relatively recently, our country was considered mission territory by the Church. It had been overwhelmingly Protestant...until the Papist "invasion" of the 1800s. Suddenly, mass immigration from Catholic countries began, and that made people nervous. The newbies had funny customs, funny food, funny clothes, and a not-so-funny religion. They had a very organized hierarchy with what was perceived as a king-like head who had a large, powerful headquarters, and even its own country. It didn't help that they had something of a *history* with the Protestants who were running this country. There were memories of wars and persecutions...and now they were coming here with their garlic, graven images, and gaggles of children. Maybe they would try and take over the country, or set new laws to make it a new Rome, or take our jobs.

We're all familiar with "Irish need not apply" and wholesale discrimination against Italians. The Catholic immigrants were relegated to ghettos, and the only work they could get was menial or dangerous labor that subjected them to horrifying, unregulated conditions. They were poor, in ill health, and unwelcome; each of these conditions reinforced by discrimination, which in turn reinforced the xenophobia of their new countrymen. The Pogues have a great song called, "Thousands Are Sailing," which shares the Irish experience of immigration to America. It's a very touching expression of the dream-crushing reality that first-generation immigrants often face, and the perseverance needed to survive and thrive despite the challenges.

For many immigrants, the Church was their haven, and priests and sisters were sent over from their native countries to minister to their spiritual needs, but also to help them navigate their new situation. This meant providing education, healthcare, and mobilization of the people to change their conditions and the laws that kept them from living in dignity.

The original story of Batman began in 1939, while the country was still trying to rebound from the Great Depression. People's lives were somewhat tenuous, and the development of Batman's character reflects the challenges of life at that time, both financial and social. All three of the Bat "family" were orphans (a common issue of the day) who, fortunately, had received excellent care from loving adults, but knew what it meant to feel vulnerable. After mobilizing to fight crime together, they mobilized to fight poverty and ignorance. Barbara worked in information technology and Bruce Wayne set up foundations in memory of his parents: The Thomas Wayne Foundation, which gave money for medical research, and the Martha Wayne Foundation, which supported orphanages, an adoption agency, and schools for poor children, and funded several soup kitchens. For them, putting bad guys behind bars wasn't the whole fight against injustice; caring for the needs of the poor was equally important.

Saints emerged in such circumstances—many women religious pioneered the education and healthcare systems that are now in place throughout the country. In the early 1800s, Elizabeth Ann Seton converted to Catholicism and was confirmed by the only Catholic bishop in the entire country—after being received in the only Catholic Church in New York. It was the only one at the time because there were laws limiting Catholic activity. She established schools to educate Catholic girls and established the first free Catholic school in the United States, focused on educating the children of the poor. Saint Katharine Drexel went beyond looking out for the Catholic minority, and took her mission to black and Native American communities in the late 1800s.

And laypeople like Dorothy Day fought for the dignity of the worker, providing assistance to the poor and raising awareness about the unjust conditions to which people were being subjected. She and other Catholic leaders were in the forefront of serving the poor and out of work, feeding the underemployed and unemployed, fighting for the dignity of the worker and the development of unions. Her legacy lives on in the publication *The Catholic Worker* and in the efforts that members of her movement continue to make in worker's rights and caring for the poor. Later, our religious leaders and laity marched with the Civil Rights Movement. Catholic social teaching requires our participation in advancing the dignity of all people. Scripture requires us to remember our past.

Many Catholic Americans of European ancestry are only third- or fourth-generation Americans and can recall their grandparent's and great-grandparent's tales of leaving the only home they knew to come to the "land of opportunity" to live the "American dream." They had it rough, and really struggled for any success that they could eke out. They were the recipients of prejudicial and unfair treatment, they were denied basic human rights, they had to huddle together for safety, and they sometimes distanced themselves as much as possible from their native culture to survive. Considering our recent past and the immigration of Latino Catholics into the United States, that line from Deuteronomy, "You shall also love the stranger, for you were strangers in the land of Egypt" (Deut 10:19), should be planted firmly on our minds, in our hearts, and on our lips. It should be a call to action for us in daily life and in the political arena.

In an episode of the TV series *Wonder Woman*, an alien named Andros from a very advanced race came to Earth to evaluate our progress—he had visited before throughout the centuries. While Andros waffled back and forth about whether humanity was worth keeping around, residents of his planet looked on and deemed us very unworthy. We were full of violence, confusion, uncharity...the list could go on. Wonder Woman tried to make a case for humanity, saying, "To work and fight for justice and democracy....I believe that's important, don't you?" We, too, can look at our countries and our world at times and wonder if there's anything redeeming. There are times when it could feel like there isn't. But our national amnesia about where we came from and how we're supposed to treat people doesn't excuse us from our call to work and fight for justice and democracy. It *is* important, and it is *our* fight.

A Voice in the Wilderness

In the tumult of Gotham, it could be very easy for anyone who was committed to fighting crime to give up. Look at the Rogues Gallery—there are more villains of every shape, size, and superpower than you can imagine. Gotham is a very dangerous city in the comic book world (it ranks seventh in a list of fifteen, which I'm certain was done in an extremely scientifically sound way). It seemed that every day a new bad guy or girl would emerge with a horrific plan to cause mass destruction, terror, and suffering. But Batman, Batgirl, and Robin faithfully plugged away, one villain at a time, taking one more danger off the streets and into the safety of an institution of rehabilitation.

The world is full of noise. Humanity's soundtrack is a constant din, a droning of opinion, marketing, diversion—many senseless sounds that keep us distracted from all we should be focusing on. Not all of it is inherently bad, it's just distracting. Evil thrives in confusion; not overly shocking confusion because that might get our attention and we might notice something's wrong; but just the right amount of confusion to keep us numb, apathetic, and believing that one person can't make a difference anyway.

So, how, if we're to be a voice for the poor, if we're to take our fight for true democracy and the dignity of all people into the public arena, can we make ourselves heard? Media is a wasteland of noise—whether spoken or written—placing us squarely in a wilderness with all the other noise. But there's some good news there...we can still be a voice crying out in the wilderness, a light in the darkness. If there wasn't wilderness and darkness, there would be no need for us to speak out. And there are some surefire ways to combat that noise. We use the voice of truth in love, and the voice of action.

The First Letter of Peter reminds us, "Always be ready to make your defense to anyone who demands from you an accounting for the hope that is in you; yet do it with gentleness and reverence. Keep your conscience clear, so that, when you are maligned, those who abuse you for your good conduct in Christ may be put to shame" (1 Pet 3:15–16). One of the biggest problems in our culture is the vitriol with which people address each other—in voice, social media, and action. The ugliness and lack of humanity they heap upon one another is the noise. If we respond in gentleness and reverence, it's music. It will be heard; it will be noticed because it's so entirely different from what everyone else is doing. We're called, as a Church, to be counter-cultural. We're supposed to be different. And, we're differ-ent—we stand out—because we live lives of radical, extravagant love. Jesus wasn't blowing smoke when he said, "Turn the other cheek." The experience of being treated with kindness when you are expecting nastiness is halting. When a person realizes that you refuse to react to them in the fashion in which they have painted you, they have two choices: to be pleasantly surprised and engage in civil dialogue, or to be indignant and remove themselves from the fight that they tried to start but have found no partner in.

Jesus made his stand within the confines of the public authority. While he spoke out against the system through his gentleness and reverence, with his words of accountability toward the leaders of the day, he also remained subject to the system. As he said when facing Pontius Pilate, "My kingdom is not from this world. If my kingdom were from this world, my followers would be fighting to keep me from being handed over to the Jews. But as it is, my kingdom is not from here" (John 18:36). He could have overthrown the Romans with no effort, but instead, he worked with what was already in place. His witness to the truth, which caused Pilate to question, "What is truth?" (John 18:38), saved the world.

Batgirl, Batman, Robin, and the Bat family worked in concert with the commissioner and the police—not trying to overthrow or undermine the system, broken as it was (and full of corruption), but working alongside it to try and improve it. Democracy isn't perfect either. We see the uncooperation and corruption daily. But it's probably the best political system on the planet. At the very least, it's one where every single citizen—and even the noncitizen—has a voice and the inalienable right to be treated with fairness and dignity. At least, that's what the Constitution says. It's the responsibility of every single citizen to be a champion of democratic laws that witness to the truth and uphold the dignity of any person who ends up in our care, however they came to be there, from conception until natural death.

Our pedigree consists of courageous heroes who, without violence, gave witness to the Catholic Christian social teachings by various paths. Some stand in undaunted silence, looking hate in the face; some write and uphold the laws that care for the poor and disenfranchised; some preach and teach the gospel; some offer direct service to the poor through social work and charitable organizations; and some pray for the rest of us. We're not all called to Batgirl's butt-kicking justice—really, none of us should go the vigilante route—but we are *all* called to hold the tension between the laws that are, the laws that should be, and the individual's dignity within the law.

CHAPTER FOUR

DOCTOR WHO

Breaking the Boundaries of Heaven and Earth

Holy, Holy, Moly

Doctor Who is a nine-hundred-year-old Time Lord who has the power of regeneration and flies around in a vessel called the TARDIS, which can transcend the parameters of space and time. The Doctor goes throughout history in the whole universe saving individuals, races, and whole planets. Here is a man who has seen everything—even the end of time and the universe. He sees how awful human beings are throughout history, but chooses to focus on the amazing good that some of them do and finds them worth saving when threatened. Even while he is horrified by their behavior, his regard for the good ones and his sense of justice keeps him in their corner.

The Doctor reminds me of God the Father. God is the infinite Creator of all, and so knows everything that ever will be. He has seen the end of all things, knows everything we will ever do (good and bad—though we never lose free will), and loves us anyway. No matter what future mistakes or atrocities we will commit, God secures our right to make them, but also the divine promise that we can be redeemed. In this chapter, let's talk about how Doctor Who can help us think about God and time.

There's an episode of *Doctor Who* called "Blink," in which the Tenth Doctor explains that time is not linear as people suppose. He says that it is instead "a wibbly wobbly timey wimey sort of thing." Some things are fixed points that can't be changed and others are negotiable. There are some points in the Christian tradition that I think many could agree would be important to remain fixed; I'm thinking especially of the birth, death, and resurrection of Jesus. Our lives don't always seem so fixed, though, and they are certainly not linear. We're learning about God all the time, and we sometimes need to rewind and think about the past to see where God was leading us even when we couldn't see the divine hand in our lives at that moment. We need, in a sense, to go back and forth in the time of our lives to see where God is leading us forward.

An episode called "The Fires of Pompeii" illustrates a fixed moment in time. The Doctor and his companion, Donna Noble, travel to Pompeii the day before Mount Vesuvius is going to blow and kill everyone in the city. As they come to know the family of Caecilius, Donna is devastated at what she knows is going to happen and begs The Doctor to do something that will alter the course of events. He can't—it's a fixed moment. The reason it must be fixed is because there were aliens in Vesuvius who were going to prevent the volcanic explosion as a by-product of their plan to conquer the world. The only way to save the world is to allow Vesuvius to complete *its* destiny and kill twenty thousand people, which simultaneously destroys the aliens. Donna and The Doctor try to warn people to flee, but they're too panicked to move. He does choose to save Caecilius's family to ease Donna's sadness, but that's all he can do.

Not all fixed events in our world are pleasant, but even the unpleasant ones have meaning. Jesus had to die so that we could have eternal life. For Christians, our personal sacrifices have meaning because they can affect the good of others—even others who are outside of time and space as we know it. Catholics pray for the dead and make little sacrifices to help them move from purgatory to heaven. Jesus's sacrifice gave meaning to ours.

We all have a general destiny—to live with God in heaven forever (if we choose it with our lives here). We have individual destinies that include lots of little destinies. For instance, one might be destined to marry a certain partner, to have kids, to be a Supreme Court Justice...that sort of thing. But the choices that person makes along the way can alter the timing, the people they meet, and the paths they'll take to get where they're going. There could be multiple potential time lines, and their choices, and the choices of others, will affect how they play out, too. It's wibbly wobbly....

Because God is eternal and exists outside of the constraints of time and space, in a sense we do, too. Everything we do has one foot in the "already," and one foot in the "not yet." There are some things that we know about the future, but there are other "spoilers" that we're not allowed to know. We celebrate what has happened before us in the history and tradition of our religious past, and we look forward to the things we know are coming, like the Second Coming, the resurrection of the body, and life everlasting.

We believe that when Jesus died on the cross and rose from the dead, and he redeemed everyone that was ever going to live, as long as they were willing to accept redemption. So, as far as God is concerned, he completed it—it is finished. No other ritual sacrifice ever needs to be made for our sins to be forgiven. God lives entirely in the already. However, many people have not been born yet, or made their mistakes and asked for forgiveness yet. Jesus conquered and obliterated sin and death on the cross—we teach this as a fact—and yet we experience those things every day. We believe that God forgives and forgets all our sins, but we still feel the effect of them. We live in the "not yet."

The way we celebrate our liturgy and salvation history has this quality, too. Take Christmas, for example. We celebrate the birth of Jesus, on one hand, knowing that it already happened two thousand years ago, and on the other hand, in some ways acting like it's happening all over again. We have Advent traditions that prepare us for Jesus to be born into our hearts anew. Some families have Nativity sets that you *wouldn't dare* put baby Jesus in before Christmas Eve. You wouldn't dare! Not because of superstition or anything, but because we "wait in joyful hope for the coming of our Savior." We're not expecting him to be born all over again as a baby, but we do experience his birth all over again at Christmas.

Then there's the Triduum: Holy Thursday, Good Friday, and Holy Saturday are the very best three days of the whole entire year. During those days, we follow the timeline that Jesus was on, observing the events in "real time." On Holy Thursday, we commemorate the Last Supper, when Jesus instituted the Eucharist/priesthood and got arrested. On Good Friday, we remember his death on the cross. Many Catholics will stop whatever they're doing at noon to say a prayer because that's when Jesus was crucified. Then we gather at three o'clock for our liturgy because that's the time he died. We read the passion like it's happening now. The community reads all the bad guy parts out loud and we feel like we're there. Then we venerate the cross, and we feel like we're there. After, we go home and continue to fast and reflect on Jesus's death like it just happened. There's a legitimate sadness in the Church that day. People bring their own emotional crosses with them as they approach Jesus's cross: widows missing their husbands, financially strapped families, children whose mother is riddled with cancer, parents assisting their adult disabled children to venerate—it's a powerful community witness and a witness to the suffering we all share in. And on Holy Saturday, we move from the darkness of the tomb to the wonderful light of the resurrection. If you've never been to an Easter Vigil, you totally need to do it. It's long, but it's the mother of all vigils.

I worked with converts to Catholicism for decades, and they receive the sacraments at the Easter Vigil Mass. The morning of Holy Saturday, we would have a retreat and celebrate some rituals to prepare them for baptism, confirmation, and their first Eucharist that will take place at the Easter Vigil, after the sun goes down (to catch us up to the third day for the resurrection). Many of the Elect (those who are going to be baptized) feel a certain sense of loss that day, remembering the people who won't be able to be there because they've passed away; often, those people were instrumental in their relationship with God that ultimately led them to the Church.

There's a particular—even peculiar—sense of time at work in the Mass. I have the privilege of explaining what happens during the Holy, Holy, the Litany of Saints, and the Consecration of the Eucharist. What happens is that the barriers of time and space completely break down; almost as if we step in to the TARDIS and sweep across the universe with the Doctor. When we sing the Holy, Holy, we join our voices to the voices of the saints and angels in heaven—that's what they sing all day, so their eternal presence enters our space. When Jesus becomes present in the Eucharist, we are not resacrificing him on the altar, but the sacrifice that he made on the cross, which is at once a fixed point in time and at the same time transcends it, catches up to us in that time and in that place; so we enter into their space. The sacrifice, the death, and the resurrection, all rolled up into one, are all truly present in the Eucharist.

The Prophet Isaiah got a glimpse of the heavenly court, describing it this way, "And one [angel] called to another and said: / 'Holy, holy, holy is the LORD of hosts; / the whole earth is full of his glory'" (Isa 6:3). The Book of Revelation provides this image: "And the four living creatures, each of them with six wings, are full of eyes all around and inside. Day and night without ceasing they sing, / 'Holy, holy, holy, / the Lord God the Almighty, / who was and is and is to come'" (Rev 4:8). They join with us and are present as we enter into the death and resurrection of Jesus that happened two thousand years ago. We call that "memorializing." When we memorialize something, it's not just remembering; it's entering into the very event as God brings it forward to us. We use their words during Mass to express the unity that we share with those who are already in heaven and those who will be born later, but already exist in their completion in the heart of God. When we sing the Litany of Saints, we call by name our friends and relatives in heaven, asking them to be with us and to help us by their prayers. We believe that they have a keen interest in us, and that they pray for us.

It reminds me of the last scene in *Return of the Jedi*. When the rebels had finally destroyed the Death Star, all the main characters are at the Ewok village on Endor, enjoying their victory over the Galactic Empire. But it wasn't just *their* victory—it belonged to others who laid the groundwork. We see (in a sort of ghostly—I'd say *resurrected*—form) Yoda, Obi-Wan Kenobi, and Anakin Skywalker. They're present at the celebration of their cooperative victory. They stood up to evil and some were killed for it, but now they're restored; and we get the sense that Anakin, Obi-Wan, and Yoda are more accessible now than they were when they were alive. In fact, we had even heard Ben speak to Luke, reminding him to "use the Force" when he's flying toward the main reactor to destroy the Death Star. Even in death, Ben helped Luke fulfill part of his destiny.

At Mass, we celebrate the victory that Christ won for us and shares with us. We also celebrate that same victory that is extended and shared by the good we do, and by the good done by those who have come before us. And they're all present at that celebration. There's no time or space; just unity. They are there with us. Though they're *out* of our time because they are in heaven, they're now also *in* our time during Mass.

The Book of Revelation offers an example. The image of the martyrs in heaven includes "they who have come out of the great ordeal; they have washed their robes and made them white in the blood of the Lamb. For this reason they are before the throne of God, / and worship him day and night within his temple, / and the one who is seated on the throne will shelter them. / They will hunger no more, and thirst no more; / the sun will not strike them, / nor any scorching heat; / for the Lamb at the center of the throne will be their shepherd, / and he will guide them to springs of the water of life, / and God will wipe away every tear from their eyes" (Rev 7:14–17).

So Mass time is timey wimey. It's like we're in the TARDIS, traveling through time and space, not bound by the rules of physics or any temporal parameters.

Prophecy

One of my favorite intersections between faith and hero stories is prophecy. It's a great coupling with destiny—we have a destiny because there was a prophecy: something needing fulfillment. The stories' villains are always aware of the prophecies, but usually laugh them off—sort of. They say they don't believe them, but *just in case*...they'll look for the special birthmark that the hero is supposed to bear, they'll employ prophets to interpret the signs so that they don't miss what they're looking for, or they'll kill thousands of innocent people to try and exterminate the hero. They go to great lengths to squelch the prophecy. But it doesn't matter what steps they take. It's a prophecy for a reason: it's going to come true one way or another.

One of my favorite examples of this is the story of *Willow*. The evil Queen Bavmorda knew of the prophecy that her reign would end when an infant bearing a special mark was born. So, she made sure that all new babies were born under the watchful eye of her henchmen. When the prophesied baby was born, a good midwife took the baby and sent her down a river to try and preserve her life. She ended up in a village of small people, at Willow Ufgood's house. Willow reluctantly accepted the responsibility of taking the infant to a big person who would make sure that she was safe. Willow, with the equally reluctant assistance of Madmartigan (a not-so-nice warrior) and the Queen's own daughter, Sorsha, rallied to overthrow the Queen. The prophesied baby had very little role in the fulfillment of the prophecy; she didn't *do* anything except to exist and be cute. Everyone else was moved into action to save the little innocent, which is what fulfilled the prophecy.

The Christian faith is based soundly in prophecy, too. We hear the stories of the infants Moses and Jesus in the Willow story: innocents are slaughtered while the key players are hidden and survive. There are events that will come to pass, one way or another, always retaining the dignity of individual free will. No one is forced to comply, but God will, one way or another, make it so. The Prophet Isaiah speaks for God, saying, "So shall my word be that goes out from my mouth; / it shall not return to me empty, / but it shall accomplish that which I purpose, / and succeed in the thing for which I sent it" (Isa 55:11).

In Scripture, the various writers were inspired to tell the people of their time what God's message was for them in that time, space, and circumstance. They didn't realize that the message they had sent at that moment and the exact wording they used would have a deeper meaning for people thousands of years later. We believe that the Holy Spirit inspired them to write it that way for that purpose. The Jewish prophets were writing for their own time, but simultaneously setting the groundwork for the Messiah, who we believe is Jesus.

In 2 Samuel, we're told that the Messiah would come from the line of David, "When your days are fulfilled and you lie down with your ancestors, I will raise up your offspring after you, who shall come forth from your body, and I will establish his kingdom. He shall build a house for my name, and I will establish the throne of his kingdom forever" (2 Sam 7:12–13). It continues, "Your house and your kingdom shall be made sure forever before me; your throne shall be established forever" (2 Sam 7:16). Nathan is telling David this regarding his own son Solomon, but it also applies to a much deeper promise—the throne forever is the one that will be established by Jesus. Isaiah remembers that prophecy and encourages the people of Israel in their dark times, saying, "A shoot shall come out from the stump of Jesse, and a branch shall grow out of his roots....On that day the root of Jesse shall stand as a signal to the peoples; the nations shall inquire of him, and his dwelling shall be glorious" (Isa 11:1, 10). Isaiah is speaking about the circumstances that Israel was facing at that specific time; but, like Samuel, he speaks of the future, too. He also gives details about what the Messiah will be like, and so much of the detail is exactly what would happen to Jesus hundreds of years later:

> For he grew up before him like a young plant, / and like a root out of dry ground; / he had no form or majesty that we should look at him, / nothing in his appearance that we should desire him. / He was despised and rejected by others; / a man of suffering and acquainted with infirmity; / and as one from whom others hide their faces / he was despised, and we held him of no account. / Surely he has borne our infirmities / and carried our diseases; / yet we accounted him stricken, / struck down by God, and afflicted. / But he was wounded for our transgressions, / crushed for our iniquities; / upon him was the

punishment that made us whole, / and by his bruises we are healed. (Isa 53:2–5)

The prophets weren't about predicting the future like fortune-tellers; they spoke in the already of what was happening right in front of them. It was their job to look at the signs of the times and see where God was present. They listened to what God had to say to the people in the present moment, and helped the people to make right choices wherever choices were to be made. Actually, we are only truly effective when we're rooted in the present moment. We can only experience reality when we're attentive to what is happening around us and we are fully engaged in and responsive to our circumstances. If we spend too much time dwelling on the past, we can get lost there, and if we spend too much time trying to guess the future, we miss opportunities now.

Kind of a neat illustration of this happened in *Doctor Who* with the running theme of the phrase "Bad Wolf." There were a series of episodes where Rose Tyler, one of The Doctor's closest companions, noticed that the phrase had been appearing in an array of times and places and languages throughout their travels—it appeared in seventeen episodes before it was finally explained. Although they had noticed it appearing in all these places, it didn't seem to have any significance until the episode "Bad Wolf," when Rose, The Doctor, and Jack from Torchwood find themselves trapped on a TV game station. The company running the programming is called "Badwolf Corporation," which makes all of the other sightings of the phrase click in her mind. As it happened, the Corporation is run by Daleks (The Doctor's worst enemy, but my favorite), and The Doctor and his companions were brought to the game station in a trap. The

Daleks intend to destroy Earth (they're always doing that...) and kill Rose and The Doctor. Naturally, that doesn't happen—The Doctor always wins. The phrase was put in all those times and places by Rose and was meant to be a warning to her and The Doctor of the presence of Daleks. He didn't know it, but it was prophetic of what he had done in the past, coming to catch up with him in the future...which eventually allowed him to change the past. Remember—time isn't linear; it's wibbly wobbly.

In the fiftieth anniversary special, "The Day of the Doctor," The Doctor finds the first version of himself on his home planet of Gallifrey at the final battle of the Time War between his people and the Daleks. He decided that the only way to end the fighting and to protect the rest of the universe from the Daleks was to annihilate both races, which would fulfill a prophecy that on the last day of the Time War, the Time Lords would die. He's going to use a weapon called the Moment, which can destroy entire galaxies. The Moment, which is also sentient and judgmental, appears to him as Rose Tyler—a companion who will become dear to him, but who he doesn't know yet. The form of Rose that it took is Bad Wolf: a powerful manifestation that Rose became when she looked into the Time Vortex of the TARDIS. Confronted with the moment that he made the decision to extinguish millions of lives, most of them innocent, he's given a new chance to make a different decision.

Another of his companions, Clara, reminds him of the meaning of his name, helping him to live up to it. Time Lords choose the name that they are known by (with another given name that they don't share often), and this Time Lord chose The Doctor. He's one who heals. His name prophesies his choice—that he will find another way to end the Time War than the one he initially chose. Instead, he freezes his planet in time and sends it to sort of another universe to hide until it can be brought back. His new choice fulfills the prophecy that Gallifrey will return after hundreds of years of having been destroyed—a prophecy that various characters speak of spanning many episodes. To me, it's a wonderful expression of prophecy; this thing is *going* to happen, but the decisions made along the way by a plethora of people in different times and spaces will affect the timing of how it will be brought about.

After a similar fashion, the way God made the first covenant with humanity and knew exactly how it would be fulfilled hundreds of years later has a prophetic element. God approached Abram and said that if Abram and his wife Sarai were open to following God, he would make them a great nation. God used the mode of covenant-making that was familiar to Abram—agreeing on terms and then sealing the deal in blood. When clans made covenants in Abram's time, there wasn't a lot of writing happening, so contracts had to be more physical. They would gather some animals, cut them in half, and separate the halves, making a lane between them. A member of each contractual party would take a stroll down the lane, which symbolized that if one broke the covenant, the other had the right to do to them and their family what had been done to these animals. In Genesis 15, God told Abram to set the animals up in this way. When night came, God put Abram into a deep sleep, and only God went down the path. This was a sign that when Abram and his descendants (us) inevitably broke the covenant—which incidentally, was that we would follow God's commandments and God would take care of us, making us a great nation—God would take all the responsibility on himself.

God knows all things. God knew we would mess up, and mess up with gusto. God knew all the terrible things we would ever do, individually and as the human race, and took the hit for us. When God made that covenant with Abram, it was already God's plan that Jesus would allow us to do to him what had been done to those animals. He completed the covenant in one historical event that echoed throughout time and space. We call it an "eternal sacrifice" because it extends forever from that fixed point when Jesus died, and also because it was completed in God's mind at the time of the covenant-making.

Bigger on the Inside

Another aspect of living outside of time and space is the vessel in which we travel. Consider the TARDIS. It looks like a police box. It looks small. It's bigger on the inside...or smaller on the outside, depending on your perspective. It is psychically and physically linked to The Doctor—they are almost sides of the same coin. And there's us. We appear very small. We appear simple to comprehend. But we're not. We're way more than we seem. We are a box, but we're also infinite. We are not limited to the box/body in which we live, but we're uniquely and eternally linked to it. God designed us to always have the body that we're given at conception and it will follow us into the resurrection when Jesus makes his second appearance here.

The TARDIS is also like Jesus (since he's a guy with a body). The Doctor's box has the appearance of something familiar to earthlings (well, British earthlings, anyway). It's a comforting sight—it represents help when you're in danger or in need of assistance. In fact, it is a functional police box, if you have the right phone number. As already mentioned, it's bigger on the inside—what's contained on the inside of the TARDIS can't even be imagined. What was on the inside of Jesus also couldn't be imagined by the people who met him. He blended in with the scenery. No one ever suspected that there was more to him than what he offered in his first thirty years of life.

But once you get a glimpse inside of Christ, you can't ever get to the end of what is contained there—infinite knowledge, moving with the changing time and events. Only there *is* a difference—instead of being adapted to the changes happening around him as the TARDIS is, Jesus is that fixed point that never changes—everything changes and shapes around him. Untold, infinite wonders are inside both. And, you only get into the TARDIS, or Jesus, by invitation. Jesus wants to reveal the mystery that is him, but not everyone can handle it, and insist on just seeing him as a man. The TARDIS is too much for some people— only some people can handle and embrace what The Doctor and TARDIS are. But even the ones who get totally freaked out by it, once they're inside, find comfort and trust.

Another aspect of Time Lords is that they regenerate. Instead of dying when they're mortally wounded, they're transformed into another form. Regeneration could speak to the way that the Church experiences time in a liturgical sense. The liturgical year is cyclical, marked by moments that we celebrate each year, but that don't land on the same day each year. Certain feasts and observances have dates attached to them, like Christmas and saints' commemorations, feast days, and solemnities, but Ash Wednesday, Easter, the new year that begins with the First Sunday of Advent, and the counting of Sundays fluctuates with nature's calendar. Ash Wednesday is forty-six days before Easter, which falls on the first Sunday after the first full moon following the spring equinox. The rest of the year falls into place according to that date because then we have forty days of Lent and fifty days of Easter, then Ordinary Time picks up. And, since we're mentioning Christmas, it's worth noting that, though we celebrate it on December 25, we don't know the exact date that Jesus was born. It's estimated from another feast—The Annunciation—that has a very ancient, fixed date of March 25... count nine months forward....

Each year ends with the celebration of Our Lord Jesus Christ, King of the Universe (previously known as Christ the King in simpler times), and the new year begins the following Sunday, the First Sunday of Advent. Each new year signals a new cycle of readings, too. We have three cycles, and each one gives us a different Gospel to focus on during the year. The readings at Mass and the prayers we pray reflect what should be happening in our personal lives as we each try to move closer in our relationship with God. We hear the same stories of Scripture every three years, but we move through them as we hear Jesus moving through his life on Earth and progressing in his mission, heading for his death and resurrection. The years of our lives flow along with the liturgical year: Advent, Christmas, Lent, and Easter being more intense periods, with Ordinary Time (meaning time that is numbered—not boring) as something of a breather, peppered with Holy Days to add a little excitement.

Lent is a time that many Christians find their spirits especially regenerated. We go into the desert with Jesus (spiritually) and empty ourselves of distractions by fasting, praying, and giving to the poor, making us ready to be filled up in the resurrection of Easter. Easter is a celebration of Jesus's resurrection, but also of the resurrection that we look forward to for ourselves.

The stories we hear in Scripture during the Easter season are the stories of the early Christian community—they are meant to encourage the newly baptized in their newfound community of faith, and each of us as we embrace the graces that we have received through our Lenten observances. We are new, and can make our community come more alive as we're all refreshed in the waters of baptism at Easter. Each liturgical year is regenerated in a slightly different form, but the essence remains the same.

So, on one hand, we amble along in linear fashion, one day moving into the next toward our final destination, and on the other hand, the way we observe and live through our liturgical year, we circle back, always being renewed and reminded of where we've been and where we're going, and we find meaning in our lives by looking at these cyclical events in relation to our own.

Regeneration is also a wonderful metaphor for the human spirit, and the Church. Trauma happens to us, around us, and in our Church family. Nothing destroys us, though. We're bigger and stronger than the circumstances inflicted upon us. In fact, very often just when it looks like we're at our breaking point—the point where nothing could possibly save us—we regroup and become something adapted, something better. We're still the same being—still the same organism with all our history and foundation—but more suited to excel within the challenges that meet us on our journey. Even when we do pass away, what we become is so much more than what we were. When we enter God's realm, we transcend time and space, become perfect and keep the relationships we have with the people who have always meant something to us—even if it does bring a period of pain and confusion to those who knew us and are still alive.

As the Catholic funeral rite says, "Our relationship is changed, not ended." The rite also says, "The ties of friendship and affection which knit us as one throughout our lives do not unravel with death." Even when we can't see the people who have gone before, the love that unites us remains intact. Love transcends time and space.

There Is No End

So, the bottom line is this—we are temporal and we are eternal. Everything is finished, and we experience an unfinished universe. Our purpose for being on this Earth is to have an opportunity to know how to love, and to choose an eternity of love. While we're trudging along what appears to be a straight line (at least in the counting of years) toward our destiny, our lives are constantly in tension between the already and the not yet.

There can be some comfort in knowing that all things will come to pass just as they should regardless of our errors, miscalculations, and flat-out bad decisions. There can be some comfort in knowing that the fate of the entire world doesn't rest on our shoulders because it's already been completed (outside of our experience). There can be some comfort in knowing that when we *do* show up, we not only touch the divine, but touch the realms of the past and future, partnering with everyone who has come before us and will ever come after us.

When I think of how God works within our time, I'm reminded of an episode of *Doctor Who* called "The Name of the Doctor." Clara Oswald is called "the impossible girl." A villain sought to undo The Doctor's actions throughout time by entering his "timestream," a column of light that exists inside of the TARDIS—remember, The Doctor and the TARDIS are inextricably linked. Seeing their success in the gradual fading of The Doctor's wife, River Song, Clara jumps into the timestream after them. She falls, much like Alice falls down the rabbit hole, interacting with different times and places where The Doctor had done significant things. As the villain undoes his actions, Clara is right behind them restoring what had been done and saving The Doctor's life. She was, in a way, working behind the scenes to make The Doctor effective where others would take his effectiveness away.

It seems to me that God works somewhat in this way. Where we would act to do good, to help bring God's salvation to others, opposing forces might try and weaken or undo our efforts. God is always quietly working behind the scenes, strengthening and giving life to even the little things we do. It reminds me, too, of prayer. We believe that our prayer has weight; it has power, because it makes us open to God's presence zipping through our timelines, bringing us help as we need it. Clara's presence in The Doctor's timeline was undetected by him. It was an act of her will to insert herself into situations where The Doctor didn't even know that he needed her. Prayer makes us more able to see God's assistance where we might have missed it before. Clara calls out to The Doctor while she's moving through his different incarnations, but he doesn't see or hear her. But as they catch up to the time when he knew her (the present in the story that we are watching), he does begin to see her. God is always with us, but it's not until we know him that we begin to recognize his help in our lives.

It was, since the moment we became part of God's imagination, God's plan that we would know him and accept his love and help. He follows each of us through our timeline, giving us strength and assistance as we need it, knowing already where we are going, what we will do, how we will succeed and fail, and when we will discover that he was always with us. God put into motion the plan for each person's salvation before we were even born; before creation was completed. He had died and rose for the sins that we would commit long before we were around to commit them.

As we ponder the mystery of our immortality and wonder how it's all possible in this world so bound by physical and natural laws that suggest that time is linear, God gives us liturgy, prophecy, and Scripture, which are touchstones to the divine. They keep us grounded firmly in the present moment and simultaneously keep us mindful of where we've been and where we're going. We have the luxury of dipping into it any time we want by picking up a Bible to read the words that, from the foundation of the Earth, God inspired to be written, so that on that day, at that moment, you or I might pick it up and experience God speaking directly to our hearts the words that we most needed to hear. We have the privilege to enter God's presence in the Mass, to break down time and space and spend time with God and everyone who ever came before or will come after us. We have the liturgical year that gives shape and color to the way we view our seasons, offering new insight through old events, with their always unfolding meaning in each new moment of our lives.

And because all of this was set in place for us before we were a twinkle in our parents' eyes, even death can't prevent our fulfilling our destiny. God gave each of us a destiny out of love. All of it was put into place—every movement, every prophecy, every bit of salvation history—so that we could experience God's love and respond in kind to it. It transcends time, space, our limitations, and our brokenness. God's goal for us is that we would experience his love for us with no boundaries whatsoever. Since we're all on different journeys, the path there can be very windy and strange. But God has been and continues to be willing to break down every barrier that would stand in our way for us to get to him.

CHAPTER FIVE

THE LANTERNS

The Most Catholic of Superheroes

An Imperfect Hierarchy

The Book of Oa, which tells the story of the people of the planet Oa, has a creation story, laws, and prophecies. It talks of the struggle between good and evil, and how the people of Oa came to reconcile their relationship to the two. They felt that there was some kind of balance needed, so some of the Oans got together to combat the chaos wrought from evil, and appointed themselves the Guardians of the Universe. Their goal was to fight for justice and peace wherever threatened. They made decisions for the universe that they *thought* were in everyone's best interests; in reality, they weren't always.

The Guardians gathered the light—each color on the spectrum—and chose the green light because it is the light of will. They felt that the strength of will was more powerful than any other emotion. They made rings that could harness the will of its wearer, making their will an extension of themselves, which transformed them into warriors of unparalleled ability. Each ring chose a wearer to become one of the Green Lanterns, and would continue to choose successors of the ring.

One of the original four who were chosen was most unexpected. Avra was a scribe for the Oans and had no apparent fighting skills; and, of course, he became the first ring-wearer to focus his will into a physical manifestation. Being a writer, he had a great imagination, and he willed a sword into existence, which led him to understand that he could will any object into existence as an extension of himself. He became known as the First Green Lantern, even though he was picked fourth (last) in the first round of picks and was the most unlikely warrior. Who would have thought that a scribe like Avra would become the model for the rest of the Green Lanterns? And yet, that's how God works, too—God frequently chooses unlikely heroes for the most important jobs, particularly leadership positions (like King David, who was very young; Peter, the first pope who denied Jesus and was a hothead; and Moses, God's mouthpiece who had a speech impediment). Avra became the first among four powerful individuals chosen to become a corps that would make its way throughout the universe, spreading justice and establishing peace. The Corps didn't act alone, though. They would always have to answer to the Guardians. There was a hierarchy right from the start. So, chosen as they were, they were still accountable.

Right off the bat, the Lanterns remind me of the Church because of their hierarchical structure; the mistakes that the Guardians made remind me of our imperfect Church with our sometimes very ugly history. Our hierarchy has certainly made decisions that weren't always the best for everyone. Sometimes, like the Guardians, they've been downright destructive. The Lanterns were subject to laws and teachings that governed their actions, and they were chosen for duty. The Prophet Isaiah wrote, "I have called you by name, you are mine" (Isa 43:1). That reminds me of how the rings chose wearers who possessed the proper disposition for their particular Corps, and sometimes their attitudes and experiences shape them for a new form of service. It reminds me of Christian vocations—God calls some to the priesthood and religious life, and some to married or single life in the secular world while also ministering to the community in the trenches.

It's also not unlike when Jesus chose the apostles to follow him. He called each personally to assist in his mission; men he knew that he could send out into the world to represent him and who would be faithful to the values that he set out for them. Apparently, it worked, because here we are over two thousand years later. They certainly had their troubles, but each brought the gospel to communities that needed Christ.

Most of all, it reminds me of religious orders; members being called for service according to their gifts and talents to most effectively serve the Church and the world. There are a ton of them and they grew organically from the service that individuals were providing to the Church. As they listened to God inviting them to change direction and deepen their ministry, new orders were born.

One of the most famous is the story of Saint Francis. Francis was a rich kid who just wanted to party. After living life as a spoiled young man, he got involved in his dad's merchant business and then tried to make a name for himself in battle. That didn't go so well. He joined the town army and their troop was devastated. He survived and was ransomed, and then thought he'd go become a knight. God told him to forget it and go home. He listened and started praying. Eventually, he heard

God tell him to "repair my church." He took it literally and tried to rebuild a local church using his dad's money. That, too, didn't go well. His dad accused him of stealing and made him renounce his relationship to his dad. So, he did.

Francis walked off into the woods and started living in extreme poverty and serving anyone he could find to serve. The Franciscans were born from him having listened to God and assisting those in need. People were attracted to his radical love in action and joined him. He didn't do what he did to accrue followers, and he wasn't trying to start a religious order; it just kind of happened. So, he made a "rule" for them to follow, which reminds me of the Lantern oaths.

While the Green Lanterns were the first formed by the Guardians, the rest of the light spectrum produced emotion-based groups, too. Sometimes they were good, and sometimes bad. Sometimes they remained in union with the original mission; sometimes they diverged in horrifying ways.

Sinestro (his name should tip you off that there's something wrong with this guy) was a Green Lantern who disagreed with the Lantern Corps' definition of justice and went rogue. He established the Yellow Lanterns, whose driving emotion is fear. They instill fear in their enemies and use it as a weapon against them. Keeping the tradition of Sinestro's dissention, the Yellow Lanterns are at odds with the Green Lanterns. An interesting parallel between the Yellow and Green Lanterns is their oaths. Each Lantern Corps has an oath whose formula is based in the formula of the original Green Corps. The Green Lanterns' oath is, "In brightest day, in blackest night, no evil shall escape my sight. Let those who worship evil's might beware my power—Green Lantern's light." Where the Green Lanterns' oath is inclusive to all their Corps, the Yellow oath ends with "Sinestro's might." He's diverged from the original, and so his Corps is personality driven instead of being driven by unity.

The Church is no novice in divergence. Individuals go rogue all the time, thinking that they know better or have a better way. Periodically, broken or selfish individuals use the Church as a means to an end—it could be as unintentional as participating in ministry as a way of searching for healing and redemption ourselves and accidentally causing harm, or it could be as diabolical as infiltrating the community in search of easy prey as food for their addiction or sickness. There's a whole industry around ex-priests who have left the authority of the Church, living as married men but presenting themselves as "married Catholic priests." They believe that they're perfectly justified in their practice when they represent themselves in this way. Unfortunately, the Catholic couples that hired them in good faith to officiate their weddings discover later, to their dismay and sometimes horror, that they had been duped—and often for a hefty price. They have made their "ministry" about themselves, which becomes harmful to those to whom they claim to minister. Siloing, schisms, and factions within parishes and even within the Christian faith seem to me works not unlike that of Sinestro.

As the Lantern spectrum began to expand, other Corps were formed and include the following: Red, which is driven by rage; Violet, which runs on love; Black, which is the power of death; White, which is powered by life. White is the combination of all colors, so any White Lantern can use the power of any of the other colors. It also has the power of resurrection. Then there's Orange. He doesn't get to be a Corps, because he's all about avarice. He is so greedy that he's perpetually afraid that everyone is out to get his Orange power, and so he just hoards it. There's no room for anyone else in his self-absorbed, addict-like mindset. His only friends are avatars of those he's killed that he uses when attacking others—which must be awfully lonely for him.

When thinking of how the Church evolves in a natural way, an example from Scripture jumps out: the conversion of Cornelius. In Acts of the Apostles 10, Cornelius, a centurion in the Roman army who was a God-fearer (a pagan who comes to believe in the Jewish God but hasn't converted) received a vision that he should send for Peter the apostle. At the same time, Peter had a vision that told him we should toss the rule of eating kosher. Peter didn't get it, and actually had to hear it a couple of times before he accepted it, but he *did* accept it. Cornelius did send some men to find Peter, who had received another vision telling him to go with the men who were coming for him. He went and preached the gospel to Cornelius and his whole household. They accepted the gospel and were baptized.

Peter came to a new awareness of what it meant to be Church from this encounter. It was bigger than the Jewish standards they had been holding their converts to. Peter said that he realized "that God shows no partiality, but in every nation anyone who fears him and does what is right is acceptable to him" (Acts 10:34–35). The community was stretched in their new understanding, but they found new gifts and a broadened range in their openness.

More Than a Feeling

One of the reasons I love the Green Lanterns so much is their dedication to will. I *get* that. Feelings can be a bit misleading at times, and left unchecked, can cause loads of harm.

Decisions based only in emotion can lead to disaster—just ask Romeo and Juliet, who abandoned their reason entirely for a less-than-week-old "love;" people on reality talk shows who may never have been master of their reason; or Kylo Ren, who appeared to be reacting childishly to some kind of perceived injustice done to him that made him kill his dad in cold blood. Dr. David Banner (if you're watching the TV show, or Bruce Banner if you're reading the comics) would love to be entirely in control of his actions but, having been overexposed to gamma rays, now battles the beast within that emerges every time he becomes hurt or enraged. He would give anything to have access to his reason and will rather than having to give it over to the Hulk, as David doesn't know what is happening when he's not in control.

If we left all our decisions up to our feelings, without calling for reinforcement from our intellect and will, terrible things would happen. In fact, they do. Relationships are often completely abandoned over some nonsense or misunderstandings based on assumptions. People retreat to the safety of walls they've built as a defense against hurt. Words are spoken hastily that can't be taken back—or won't be taken back—and won't be forgotten. Murders are committed; "crimes of passion" wound our world because people give up their will for what they feel will satisfy them in a fleeting moment. Naturally, it doesn't, and the scars of uninformed, unchosen actions—reactions—prevent them from finding peace.

There was a story about a woman of color whose son was murdered by a white supremacist. Rather than seeking vengeance, the grieving mother looked for justice, and as a Christian who didn't believe in the death penalty, tried to have it removed as an option for the punishment of her son's killer. She failed. He was given the death penalty and put on death row. She wrote him comforting letters, telling him that she forgave him and was praying for him. She visited him in prison. When the time came for his execution, the person he wanted to talk to before he died was this woman—she'd become something of an adoptive mother to him.

Many people, if asked what they'd do if their child was treated unjustly, never mind murdered, say that they would seek revenge. Our immediate response is to inflict the pain that we or our loved ones have received. But that's not what we're called to. We're called, as that mother did, and as Jesus did, to find understanding and work very hard at forgiveness. After Jesus's night and day of torture, which culminated in his unjust crucifixion, as he hung dying, Jesus's response was, "Father, forgive them; for they do not know what they are doing" (Luke 23:34). And it's natural to say, easy for him—he's God. But countless saints have done the same; Saints Peter, Maria Goretti, and Thomas More, to name a few.

Saint Thomas More had lots of time to think about the injustice that he was being subjected to. While he was waiting in the Tower to be beheaded, he wrote advice on "How to Treat Those Who Wrong Us." It was probably his way of processing his own feelings in the face of injustice and imminent death, but he made one of his final acts an offering to help others in the same position. He's so cool. His sense was that people can change. If they remain bad, that's up to them, and they should be pitied and prayed for. But if they did change, the two of them would wind up being buddies in heaven because there's no hate there. He kept a cool head, as it were, and rather than stewing and breathing venom against Henry (who was supposed to be his friend), he used his time and his rational mind to become more like Jesus.

One of our greatest gifts is our will, and it shouldn't be underestimated. Our free will—our ability to learn, comprehend, and use our intellect to make whatever choices belong to each of us—is what makes us unique individuals. God made us in God's image and likeness, giving us the ability to love. That love isn't a feeling—it's a choice. Love can't be demanded or required, it can't be engineered or manufactured. It is a free act of the will. Of course, we may *feel* love toward another, but to act on that feeling: to offer gifts, create art or poetry, to seek a deeper connection or union with the other—each is an act of the will. If an individual isn't free to choose their response in any given relationship, then the relationship isn't a love relationship.

It's not right to underestimate feelings, either; feelings are good and useful. Take the feeling of guilt, for example. People generally think of guilt as a bad feeling; especially when associated with the Catholic Church. It does *feel* bad, but it's not evil. Guilt is a signal that something's not right. Guilt tells me that I've done something wrong, and that my actions need to be addressed. But I'm not meant to remain in the feeling of guilt my whole life. If I'm using guilt correctly, I'll take inventory of my actions and right my wrong, which will alleviate my guilt. The same goes for anger, joy, confusion, sadness, peace, contentment—each of which is an opportunity to discover how on track my actions are, or how other people's actions are affecting me.

Our will helps us to govern our passions, and gives us the gift of reason when we might otherwise be ruled by feelings. To step out of the comic book world for a second, let's take a diversion to space, that final frontier. My favorite Vulcan, Spock, is unique among others of his race. He's half Vulcan and half human. In a way, the poor guy's Vulcanness has been somewhat sabotaged by his genetic makeup. The Vulcans used to be an extraordinarily passionate bunch. They were ruled by emotions and, as a result, got into all kinds of trouble. Over the centuries, they worked at curbing their emotions, trying to weed them out entirely from their being. Now, poor Spock becomes a throwback, having his cool, scientific, passionless self in control at all times—almost. And I'm not just talking about the Pon farr; he has his human moments where feelings tend to surface. In the TV episode "The Enemy Within," Spock talks about how a war wages within him because he's half human and half Vulcan, but that he survives because his intelligence wins out. Suppressing his emotions through use of his intelligence is really an exercise of the will. It helps him to be logical in situations where McCoy or other crewmen might behave hastily.

The Guardians have it right—will is the most powerful force (even if they *do* call it an emotion). When we use it correctly, we become more divine, more in line with the power of God. We believe that the more we exercise our will for good, the freer our actions become. Saint Ignatius developed a form of prayer called the Examen that all Jesuits are required to practice because it's aimed at developing freedom of will. The point of it is to set aside quiet time to place yourself in a state of gratitude, to ask God to walk with you through the events of your day, to explore the feelings and thoughts (briefly) you encountered as a result of the events, to evaluate your responses or reactions, and to ask God to help you make better choices next time where the ones you made weren't in perfect freedom. The assumption is that we can be perfectly free if we use our will to respond to our circumstances (driven by exercising our will) instead of reacting to them (driven by emotion). And, as with all things, practice makes perfect.

The thing about will is that, if you develop a strong one, no one can take it away from you. No one can force another person to do anything. If one knows what's right and is committed to the truth, their will prevails over any evil. Like Jesus, it might not always look like a victory because the result may be forfeit of life; but, ultimately, the choice to do no wrong is the choice for true life.

As strong and important as will is, it's nothing without some direction. An unrestrained, unaffected will can be as destructive as one driven by a well-formed conscience can be healing. And so, for direction, we need things like faith, hope, and love. Saint Paul would say that "the greatest of these is love" (1 Cor 13:13), and he'd be right (I'm not going to challenge Paul), but we already talked a lot about faith and love, so I'd like to talk about hope.

The Blue Lanterns began when a Green Lantern named Saint Walker (awesome name!) was feeling really beaten down by the successes of the Red Lanterns and went to a sentient planet named Mogo. (He's a planet that has self-awareness, a will and the ability to talk and move out of his orbit). Saint Walker was looking for the answer to "Who is the Savior?" He believed that there was one who could defeat the Red Lanterns, but he didn't know who. Mogo told him, in response to his question, "Climb." Distracted by the arrival of Red Lanterns, Saint Walker wants to go after them. Mogo tells him that his path is not revenge—he needs to use his will to keep walking. He had to go on a mini-quest to the top of the mountain to discover that the answer was hope, and the answer was himself. He's convinced that if he can believe, then he can make a difference. He joins the Green Lanterns, who are engaged in battle with the Red Lanterns, as a newly minted, first of his kind: Blue Lantern. Adding his hope to their will (along with Mogo—that sentient planet), they become strong enough to defeat the rage of the Red Lanterns.

In a way, while it was Saint Walker's revelation that changed him into a Blue Lantern, he didn't do it alone. It was the prompting of Mogo that led to Saint Walker's discovery of the hope he kept in his heart. We all need a Mogo to invite us to climb. I would compare the wisdom and movement of Mogo to the Holy Spirit. Sometimes, as with Saint Walker, we need to have our will challenged for it to grow or to find the strength to wield it. That strength has only one source—hope. Hope is the driving force that makes us believe that what we do matters, that our actions can be truly free and effective, and that we can become something better than what we began as. We need hope to inform and form our will.

Pick a Color

In many ways, we're like the Lanterns. We might have been chosen for some specific destiny—to protect and serve a group of people, to minister to a community, to share a particular gift or talent; we may have committed ourselves to live a certain lifestyle through the promises we make in marriage, or holy orders, or as members of secular orders, or as members of religious communities.

We pray the Nicene Creed, our "rule" or "oath," as a battle cry for how we'll live our faith as individuals and as community. There's a Latin phrase regarding prayer, "lex orandi, lex credendi," which means, "the law of praying, is the law of believing." We pray the words that our community believes and it instructs us as to what the Church teaches. Like the Lanterns, our oath simultaneously defines and reminds us of who we're supposed to be. We pray it together as community because, as people chosen for one another, we share those beliefs. Each point in the Creed begins "I believe..." because each point is for every individual to live personally. The Lanterns call out their oaths for their own hearing, renewing their sense of duty and purpose, and as a warning to those with whom they'll do battle. It's a sign of their identity, their values, and their action plan. The same is true for us.

As people of faith, we engage our feelings as we navigate the world that God created for us. If we can learn to interpret our feelings and use them appropriately, everything we do will go much smoother. I think of the story of the Road to Emmaus—the disciples acknowledge that as they were listening to their companion speak, their hearts were "burning within" them (Luke 24:32). The story goes that, after Jesus had died and then was discovered to be missing from his tomb, the apostles and disciples were properly dismayed. They didn't know what to think of it. Mary Magdalene had found Jesus missing from the tomb and was told by an angel that he was alive; she told the apostles this news, but the community didn't know what to do with that information. In fact, everybody but Peter thought it "seemed to them an idle tale" (Luke 24:11). They didn't know how to process it. Two of the disciples, after hearing that story, went for a walk and were joined along the way by Jesus, but they didn't recognize him. He explained everything to them as they walked, and when he was going to take his leave from them, they begged him to stay—they were drawn to him and what he had to say, but their feelings of sadness and confusion prevented them from understanding their intuition. It wasn't until he broke bread with them and blessed it that they realized he was Jesus.

It's an interesting story because their feelings are conflicted, and therefore simultaneously working for and against them. But in their heart of hearts, they recognized God's presence in the words they were hearing. If they had trusted their heartburn (the good kind), their eyes would have been opened to Jesus right in front of them long before. I could feel the facepalm that Jesus must have wanted to do when he said to them, "Oh, how foolish you are, and how slow of heart to believe all that the prophets have declared! Was it not necessary that the Messiah should suffer these things and then enter into his glory?" (Luke 24:25–26). I mean, really—how many times did Jesus tell them that those exact things were going to happen? He told them repeatedly that he would suffer and die, and we know they heard him because they got in trouble when they responded to his claim. If they had trusted the feeling deep in their hearts; the one that was stronger than the others, and used their memory to support their feelings, they would have figured it out right away. Their will to understand kept their heads in the game, and eventually they could digest the spiritual food that Jesus was giving them. Their feelings were validated, and their minds were enlightened.

Many Christians are feeling-driven, which, like the guys on the road to Emmaus, can be useful. They're sparked by a profound sense of gratitude: a belief that everything they have, they received as free gift from God. They make their lives a gift to others moved by this gratitude. That's awesome. That kind of self-giving is always renewed because it's rooted in joy.

But not all Christians have the warm, fuzzy feelings to guide them, and rely even more heavily on their will. For some, faith is almost entirely an act of the will. Saint (Mother) Teresa of Calcutta wrote about her feelings of emptiness and doubt, wishing to feel the love of Jesus, but the feelings simply weren't there. Long stretches of her life were particularly challenging because of this. At some points, her work was driven entirely by her will to serve God through the poor in front of her, even though it didn't come with the feelings of accomplishment and satisfaction that accompany so many of our good deeds. The strength of her will was an amazing testament to her faith.

Every Christian moves through "dry periods" where they have to rely on their intellectual faith to carry them through the desert. If a faith is based only in feeling, it's going to falter eventually, because feelings are fleeting. If a faith is entirely intellectual and doesn't touch the heart at all, it can eventually grow cold. Just as our feelings need tempering, our intellect and will do. We can't rely on either side exclusively.

How many marriages, or vocations to the priesthood, or school years, or jobs have times when the participants are just coasting? All of them! We don't always *feel* it. How often do grieving people, or addicted people, or terminally ill people, or new mothers deprived of sleep make it through a day because they willed it? Sometimes the only thing that keeps one foot moving in front of the other is the will to keep moving. It's especially then that our will is a gift.

We shouldn't underestimate the gift that those dry periods can be for us. Every Lent we're invited into the desert with Jesus to prepare us for the nourishing waters of baptism at Easter. Desert times are moments where everything extra is stripped away, times of reflection, thirsting, and growth. They're a time for us to confront our brokenness face to face, or to discover what's missing from our lives—what our deepest longings are so that we can let God fill them.

One of my favorite authors in the Bible is the prophet Jeremiah. He was depressed. Sometimes he was morbidly depressed. In one of his conversations with God, he lays into the all-powerful Creator, venting all his anger at him. He feels like God duped him into his ministry—he was born into a family of priests, and instead God called him to be a prophet to his enemies. It didn't go well. He often wishes he was never born and wants to give up. Lots of people can relate to that feeling. After Jeremiah rails about feeling misled by God, his deepest sense is revealed, "If I say, 'I will not mention him, / or speak any more in his name,' / then within me there is something like a burning fire / shut up in my bones; / I am weary with holding it in, / and I cannot" (Jer 20:9).

Jeremiah's an emotional guy, but most of his emotions are negative. Amazingly, that doesn't make him a bad prophet. He's moved to respond to the call God gave him because the truth that he was entrusted with is bigger than his dismal disposition. This Puddleglum must plug along—he doesn't have the luxury of quitting because his will rallies and overtakes his sadness.

If Jeremiah was a Lantern, he'd probably be a Green one. Then again, if Jeremiah was a Lantern, the Northern Kingdom of Israel would need to have watched its step. Jeremiah, Saint

Teresa of Calcutta, and so many other saints were burdened with less than cheerful dispositions. There was still a place for them. Our feelings, while important, don't define us. Our actions do. We can all be like the Lanterns and let God use what we *do* have for his glory. If our feelings are lacking, we can use our will. If we have the gift of hope, we can blow that up, let it be our strength, and make it a beacon for others.

And, if we don't have a ring to accentuate our gifts, that's okay. We have prayer. A ring would be cool, though. But prayer is good, too. It gives us strength and gives life to the gifts we have. I could be an Avra: an overlooked underdog who has imagination enough to be open to God's plan for me, or I could be a Saint Walker, who doesn't accept that what's in front of him is all there is and finds hope in his challenge. But a good prayer life includes discernment—being attentive to what God wants to do in your life. If you don't know which Corps you belong to, listen. And if you're in a Corps that doesn't seem to suit you, climb higher. Whatever you do, ask yourself and ask God what color you are. Find the Corps that you can serve.

CHAPTER SIX

VILLAINS

God's Not Done with Them Yet

What Makes a Villain

Sometimes I find supervillains more interesting than heroes. I'm all for truth, justice, and the American way, but villains are tantalizing. Many actors prefer playing a complex villain to a one-note good guy or girl for those very same reasons. Heroes have their internal struggles, but they have done more of the "work" toward healing than villains have (for the most part). Even if they aren't moving toward healing, at least the hero is making good life choices...or if not especially good life choices, at least they are working toward the good of others.

Often, the only observable difference between a hero and a villain is that the hero serves others and the villain serves his own selfishness. Both villains and heroes often have terrible backstories that led them to the paths they are on; they both tend to struggle with unresolved feelings and issues. And they both have amazing potential. It's just what they choose to do with it that makes them different. Because there are such similarities between the hero and the villain, the villain evokes a pity and sympathy—because it really could have gone either way—

and some heroes are just ticks away from supervillainy themselves. As Doctor Xavier says in *X-Men: Days of Future Past*, "Countless choices define our fate. Each choice, each moment; a ripple in the river of time. Enough ripples and you change the tide: for the future is never truly set."

Each of us is responsible for our own destiny—and our worst moment doesn't have to (and *shouldn't*) define us. Any one of us could go the *wrong* way, and at any moment any villain could go the *right* way. Besides, without villains, there's no need for heroes—they make opportunities for heroes to emerge and give them a purpose.

In one insightful episode of the Fox network's *Batman: The Animated Series* called "Trial," Batman was accused by the district attorney during a press conference of having created the villains that he spent his time capturing. Latching onto this, the inmates of Arkham, the insane asylum of Gotham, captured Batman and put him on trial, trying to make him responsible for their criminal activity, along with the district attorney, who is forced to be his defense attorney. I found that episode particularly compelling. I don't know what this says about me, but I wondered if a couple of their accusations made a little sense. They had me wondering for a short while if *some* of what Batman was doing could have contributed to their villainy. Of course, this would have been no excuse for their terrible behavior, but I wondered if he didn't sort of feed into their insanity a little bit.

His attorney's argument was that *they* had, in fact, created *him*, not the other way around, and that they would have turned out as they did (except probably dead) if Batman hadn't been there. When the arguments close, the Joker, who acts as judge, finds Batman "not guilty." He's nuts, but he's got at least *that* level of self-awareness.

This episode brings to my mind the story of Jonah. Jonah was a prophet of Israel, at the top of his game, to whom God had given a hard job—to go to his enemies (the people of Nineveh) and warn them that if they didn't change their ways (stop worshipping idols) they would be destroyed. Jonah didn't want to save them, and took a detour. He tried to sail away to the opposite end of the Earth to avoid his calling. While he was on his voyage, a great storm arose and threatened to destroy the ship. He told the crew to throw him overboard so that they would be spared—he realized that God made the storm to get him back on track. A large "fish" swallowed Jonah and the storm stopped, saving the ship and its crew. Inside the fish, Jonah had an experience of mercy and promised to do what God asked of him. After three days, the fish spat him onto landlocked Nineveh (seriously talented fish), where Jonah completed the mission God gave him. And then Jonah went up on a hill to wait for their destruction. He didn't believe that God would save his enemies. After waiting around a bit and becoming dehydrated, he began to get angry. God gave him shade for a while, and opportunity to apply the lesson that if *he* could be forgiven, so could *his enemies*, but he rejected it all. Only one outcome would be acceptable to him—the destruction of Nineveh. He got so angry he wanted to die.

Jonah reminds me of the villains in this story. They're all brilliant—they all had potential for terrific careers and to do much good in society. If you pay attention to their backstories, many of them *did* start out as exemplary citizens; and even employees of Wayne Industries. But then they were inflicted with a hurt or anger from which they could not, or would not, recover. Given chance after chance to repent, they did not. They'd rather risk their lives and others' proving that they were right to be villains because life isn't fair. Like Jonah, they attack the guy who gives them the opportunities to change. The villains blame Batman for the mess they're in because he reflects truth to them. He makes it uncomfortable and challenging for them to persist in their chosen way of life.

God's response to Jonah when he interiorly puts God on trial is this: "And should I not be concerned about Nineveh, that great city, in which there are more than a hundred and twenty thousand persons who do not know their right hand from their left, and also many animals?" (Jonah 4:11). Batman didn't *make* the people he protects, and he didn't make the villains, though they would try and claim for a time that he did. But he sees the villains the way that God sees the people of Nineveh; flawed, in need of instruction and rehabilitation, and with a hope that they will someday be made right.

Batman *is* a standup guy—one of my favorite things about him is the dignity with which he treats criminals. He never used excessive force, and never wanted to kill anyone. He showed incredible compassion for the criminals (the foundation for which is beautifully introduced in the series *Gotham*), and it was clear that besides defending Gotham, his goal was to get them help when there could be help for them. In this animated series, his empathy toward the individuals whom he must stop is clearly illustrated, episode after episode. He would try to reason with the ones who weren't completely insane, but were just off track. He tried to help them make better decisions and to get back on track before their actions proved too dangerous to let them walk away. When I remembered Batman's compassion, I acquitted him of any wrongdoing. Ironically, the villains did, too. Naturally, being psycho villains, they try to kill Batman and the district attorney anyway. And, naturally, Batman saves his life and hers and puts everything back in order.

In real life, this is a legitimate concern—our actions, even when our intentions are good, can cause harm to others. All too often, parents seeking to protect their children from hurt, minor failures, unpleasant realities of life, making mistakes, or taking responsibility for mistakes they've made (making it someone else's fault) prevent them from learning valuable lessons or even growing up. In our zeal to be a hero, we can really injure those that we perceive as a threat. Or, in our day-to-day dealings with people that we find aggravating, annoying, rude, or disrespect-ful, the way we either respond or react to them can have a last-ing effect on them.

Making Good Choices

Consider Darth Vader. He's got a pretty sad story. And the way it was told in the prequels to the original Star Wars movies was even sadder (because they were awful). He was a Jedi who was brought up too soon—wise Yoda said he wasn't ready, but Obi-Wan wouldn't listen. He trained him and made him a Jedi before he was mature enough to deal with the Force appropri-ately. The Force was very strong with him, and he had great potential in so many areas, but he probably really didn't have the temperament to be a Jedi. In the most vulnerable moment in his journey, while he was struggling with his emotions, some ter-rible things happened that made him decide his course. Bad people drew him in the direction of his more natural inclinations toward anger and lack of trust, which, had they been overcome, could have been converted to strengths. Then he was faced with the death of his wife and thought that his child died (he didn't know about the twin daughter). He further indulged his negative leanings by believing lies told to him about his culpability in the death of his young family and that he could never be forgiven. He gave up his free will and went to the Dark Side to "do his master's bidding." His physical debilitation is indicative of his interior, spiritual, and emotional debilitation. He relies entirely on artificial means for survival. He is not in control of himself—he is more machine than man. He has lost most of what makes him, him. And the worst part is that he handed it over. He gave it up. He relinquished his will to one who would devour it and remove as much of his personhood as he could. That really is the Dark Side.

When he meets his son, Luke Skywalker, he believes—and tries to convince Luke—that Luke's destiny is to evil, too. Lucky for Luke, he had better help in Obi-Wan (who was much older and wiser now) and believed that good would always defeat evil. By the time Luke meets Ben Kenobi (Obi-Wan), Ben has benefited from the wisdom that comes from experience and reflection. He is no longer the headstrong Jedi who accidentally helped create Darth Vader. He is the calm, kind, contemplative mentor who knows that the Force is not destroyed in death. He gives up his own life in battle to gain time for Luke and company to escape. Although Luke was devastated by Ben's sacrifice, it was further proof to him of the truth of the goodness of the Force. Luke didn't give in to the temptation of the Dark Side and chose the more difficult way—the light way of the Force.

The Force and the Dark Side are attractive because they are different sides of the same coin. The Force is in everyone, but depending on how we live and the attitudes we adopt, it can be light or darkness. We are spiritual people. Spirit has only one origin—God—but depending on the way *we* choose to live and the attitudes *we* adopt, we can let our spirit reflect the image and likeness in which we were made (light) or to reject it— rejecting the gift of ourselves—and dwell instead in deeper and deeper darkness, where we let others decide our fate.

One of my favorite chapters in the whole Bible is Wisdom 17. It tells what happened in Egypt during the ninth plague: darkness. This wasn't normal darkness; this was a "darkness that can be felt" (Exod 10:21). During this darkness, the Egyptians were plagued by the terror of the false gods they worshipped. They had given themselves over to craven, angry, self-serving gods, and their imagination of the evil that accompanied them was overwhelming. Every tiny sound of crickets or gentle breeze struck new horror in their hearts: "They were seized, and endured the inescapable fate; / for with one chain of darkness they all were bound. / Whether there came a whistling wind, / or a melodious sound of birds in wide-spreading branches / ...it paralyzed them with terror" (Wis 17:17–19). They gave their reason away in favor of the darkness by handing over their fates to gods that didn't care about them—gods that weren't even real. Their fear brought them deeper into isolation, where they looked for comfort but only found a more profound fear. It didn't have to be that way. "For the whole world was illumined with brilliant light, / and went about its work unhindered, / while over those people alone heavy night was spread, / an image of the darkness that was destined to receive them; / but still heavier than darkness were they to themselves" (Wis 17:20–21). That is the brilliance of evil; it convinces the subscriber of the lie that "in their secret sins they were unobserved / behind a dark curtain of forgetfulness" (Wis 17:3), but it only alienates them from themselves and others and hides from them any hope of redemption.

It becomes clear in his dialogues with Luke that Darth Vader is locked in a struggle within himself. He's not entirely devoid of love, and while he clings to his belief that he's beyond redemption, it's love that calls him back to himself. He becomes his own master again when he sees his son refuse to buckle to the temptation of despair the way he did when he was young. He sees in Luke the virtue he lacked and is inspired to recall what he once had been. For all the evil he has perpetrated throughout his lifetime (even toward his own son), he sees that he can be forgiven (even if only by his son) and chooses to be forgiven and to be free. As Darth Vader lays dying, Luke says, "You're coming with me. I'll not leave you here, I've got to save you." His father replies, "You already have, Luke. You were right. You were right about me. Tell your sister...you were right." As he lay dying, he embraces the salvation that was always available to him. And he hopes to be reconciled with his daughter (whose planet he destroyed and who he personally tortured to get information about the rebels). His hope is restored and he is himself again.

Finding Yourself

Another intriguing villain is Marvel's version of Loki, God of Mischief. You have to feel for Loki. He was an Ice Giant taken as a spoil of war to be raised by Odin as his son. Growing up different from everyone around you without understanding why you are different would be confusing and depressing for anyone. It would be very isolating to think that you *should* fit in, and yet something about you *doesn't* fit in. Being shown up by your brother every day would be, too. Loki never felt he measured up, and no matter how hard Odin tried to treat him as he did Thor, Odin knew what Loki really was, which made him suspicious and wary of Loki. Odin would never be able to look at Loki the way he looked at Thor.

Can you imagine finding out that you were adopted by your people's enemy? To find out that you aren't even the same species as your parents—or anyone on your planet—could be seriously distressing. It would explain a lot about the feelings he had and never understood. Now, Loki could have responded, "Wow. That was nice of Odin to save me from almost certain death or evil." Superman responded that way. But it is not completely out of the realm of understanding that Loki didn't. And we see that he isn't exactly *bad*...he's *mischievous*. Mischievous like a guy who tries to get rid of his brother, risks his adopted dad's life, and joins himself to vengeful members of his own race to make himself look like a hero. He's the kind of guy who likes to do bad things simply because they're bad (we all know people like that). But he's not quite *evil*. He's broken. He wants to be accepted; he wants to be great; he doesn't want to disappoint his adopted mom—he sincerely loves her, so how bad could he be? Anybody who loves their mom must have *some* redeemable qualities. And so, he does do some good.

When Loki tries to subjugate humanity, it stems from his desire for respect and validation—to feel like he matters. He couldn't get that on Asgard in his current situation. He also wanted his brother to see his worth. He needed to prove his worth to himself, too, and the only way he thought he could do it was to find success in leadership. Unfortunately, the model of leadership that he chose was megalomaniacal. He knew it was wrong, but he didn't have the confidence or the proper set of circumstances to do it the right way. Did I mention that he loved his mom? That goes a long way. Plus, he *did* help Thor when things with the Dark Elves got hairy. There was some redemption for him.

We see his good and natural desires twisted by disappointment and despair. He doesn't have hope of being loved for who he is by his family; he has no hope of being respected or acknowledged as a son of Odin. And, since his mom was killed (and it was *kind of* his fault) the only place he finds any hope is in being needed by his brother, Thor. Periodically, Loki reflects some of the decency and even love that has been instilled in him by loving parents and a brother who *never* gives up on him.

Then there's Magneto. He had a power that the absolute wrong people wanted to exploit when he was at an extremely impressionable age. His story begins in World War II, where, having been brought to a concentration camp, the Nazis discovered his ability to manipulate metal with his mind. They attempted to manipulate him into working for them. They shot his mother right in front of him, convincing him it was his fault in order to break his poor little brain and make him believe that he had no choice but to work for them. This began the path toward fear, anger, and self-hatred that would shape his worldview.

Even though he was given a chance to learn a better way to live through his interactions with a shamelessly hopeful Charles Xavier—to accept kindness and to be taught compassion for others—scars made so deep when one is so young are hard to recover from. He would always have that trauma moving and forming him—the shame of being unable to save his mother, the sense of helplessness, fear, and distrust. He worked with Xavier to try and help mutants like himself to find normalcy, to have a safe place to grow and learn and to become useful members of society because, at some point, he believed it was possible. But when he was faced with the terror of persecution and attempted annihilation, he defaulted to meeting violence with violence—terror with terror. He relapsed to what, in his young life, was most formatively a part of him. But it wasn't truly his nature, as we see later. Being hunted as a freak and a villain when you're just trying to be nice can have a profound effect, and when horrible people convince you at a young age that you are, in fact, a freaky villain, trusting in the more recently introduced kindness and mercy could be an insurmountable task. It's a pitiable situation.

Hope for the Forsaken

These are just a few examples of villains who were created by the cruelty or neglect of others. The authors of comic books, novels, and movies tell us villains' stories because they resonate with us and so we can be invested in their characters—they don't just randomly show up one day for no reason and try to take over the world. There's always something that went wrong in the villain's life to get him to that point. We're meant to feel for them; surely to hope that they're defeated, but maybe to hope that they can be converted, too.

The heroes certainly hope for it. They go way out of their way to *not* destroy the villains—they seek justice with mercy. It's usually necessary to beat the snot out of them first, but that's just self-defense. Ultimately, they offer them a chance to repent, and they want to imprison, not kill, them when they're finally subdued. From a Catholic Christian perspective, it's a very pro-life approach. We teach respect for and protection of life in every stage, regardless of whether the individual "deserves" it, hoping that gentle correction will encourage them toward repentance and reconciliation. Sometimes, after the pain that villains cause, it can be a struggle for the hero to not destroy them, but they recall that the difference between them is the ability to show mercy. Plus, how very often has it happened that the mercy shown in leaving the bad guy alive wound up being helpful—even Earth-saving (or Middle-earth–saving! I'm looking at you, Sméagol!).

I remember watching shows when I was a kid—Adam West's *Batman*, *The Incredible Hulk*, *Wonder Woman*, any super-hero show (or James Bond movie)—and wondering why the villains always revealed their whole plot before setting up the machine that's going to kill the hero in their absence. If you want to kill someone, you've got to make sure they're dead—not walk away and leave it to chance—they're heroes for God's sake—they'll escape! Every child has made this observation: what stops villains from realizing this?! Villains are their own worst enemy. They sabotage their own success repeatedly.

Is it hubris? Yes. But I think it's also a deep-seated desire to fail. Nobody *wants* to be evil. Villains always attempt to rationalize their descent into the dark alley of evil in their backstory monologues. Why? Because they like to hear themselves talk? Probably. I do that sometimes. But more to the point, they have someone good in front of them. They're challenged by that goodness—not only are their *plans* challenged, they *themselves* are challenged. They need to explain how they got to where they are because they really don't want to be there. It's unnatural to them. It's abhorrent. They either want to be justified or forgiven. And the things they say to the hero—oh the things they say! They are very provoking. It can't be *just* to taunt them. But even taunting has a purpose. It's to get a reaction—and what sort of reaction does a villain want if he (or she) has the hero just where he wants him? Is anger enough? Is the feeling of failure enough? Regret? Humiliation? Surely the villain undoubtedly wants the hero to feel all the things that he has felt throughout his life that got him to that point, but to what end? The villain wants to be understood—he wants empathy. No matter how broken we are, we're never beyond wanting empathy. It is so natural and so hardwired into us to want to be known—even for villains.

Although he wasn't a *villain* as such, Job was the king of monologues. One of the oldest and most interesting stories in the Bible, the story of Job is one of terrible misfortune. Job (like many villains in comic books) was a good guy—minding his own business unless someone came to him for advice—who had become wealthy and had a big, beautiful family. Satan (who here is understood as more of a nasty lawyer in God's court than the devil we think of today) went to God and said that he bet he could make a good guy turn bad. God said, "No way," and, "Try Job." They set some ground rules and the bet was on. Satan killed everyone in his family except his wife (so she could nag him) and destroyed everything he had. He got sick, was covered in boils, and was left destitute.

A few of his friends popped by to try to comfort him, but instead of accepting their comfort, Job plays out the stages of grief right in front of us. He's confused, in disbelief, angry...he does it all. Naturally he then starts blaming God. Nothing can convince him that it will work out okay and he spends forty-one of the forty-two chapters refuting his friends in a monologue about how unfair God is. Unlike Jonah, there's a happy resolution for Job. His monologue pays off, because for him, it's a path to understanding. If Job had closed himself to the truth, he would have done exactly what Satan had intended and he could have become a villain—not necessarily a Joker type, but in his heart, he could have become truly bitter, resentful, and corrupt. But he was eventually open, and his openness restored him.

Nobody is born evil, and nobody, in their heart of hearts, wants to be. The villain craves wholeness as much as the rest of us do. It seems unattainable to him because he has ventured so far down the wrong path. Do you see a common theme in them? They are repeatedly lied to. Sometimes they lie to themselves, but more often they're lied to by someone who seeks to exploit them. It's hard for a decent person to believe that the bad things they've done can be forgiven, never mind forgotten. How can a villain have a normal life after the havoc they've wreaked?

Let's pause for a moment to note that we've come to the true difference between heroes and villains—hope. Deep down, heroes believe that good might prevail, that wholeness and justice are possible—they have hope. Hope for humanity, for themselves, and in some cases (I'm thinking particularly of Batman and Doctor Xavier, here) for the villains with whom they battle. Heroes manage to find some sort of forgiveness in their hearts and so believe that others can also forgive. Heroes take their troubles and channel them into getting justice for others, even when they can't get justice for themselves. They choose to believe that justice is possible. The villain has no hope. He doesn't believe that justice is a real thing. It doesn't exist for him so it doesn't exist for anyone else, either. He can't forgive the hurts that he's experienced, and therefore doesn't believe that anyone could ever forgive him.

This lie is the same lie that every human being, at some point, is lulled into believing, even if for a short time. The enemy of God wants people to believe they're not worthy of love and can't be forgiven. He wants people to have no hope. This plays right into the devil's wheelhouse, because where isolation lives, he thrives. All it takes is the seed of doubt, which, when nourished, grows into self-hatred, loneliness, paranoia, and acting out. Truth, however, never lets the lie go unchallenged. The villain sees what he thinks is folly in the hero's attachment to others (even strangers) and is confounded by it. It has weight—it's effective, unfailing, and freeing. Eventually, the villain must decide whether he will give it a try or lose himself completely. He must decide whether he can discover any evidence in the case for hope.

This is true for all of us. When we sin, we believe several lies. We believe that our happiness is more important than that of others. We believe that the activity in which we're indulging will make us happy (it won't). We believe that our actions don't matter. And we can eventually come to believe that *we* don't matter, that we aren't really loved, and that we can never be forgiven.

We also have to decide who we will listen to—the loud voice that screams lies at us, or the quiet, persistent voice that tells us to come home and be restored. Sometimes it can be harder to see the evidence of hope, but if we trust it even a little, it grows and grows.

The choice to allow ourselves to be redeemed is why the most satisfying stories are the ones in which the villain gains his life back, partly because it's in our nature to want everyone to find redemption, and partly because it always happens through a loving interaction. In our Christian tradition, many of the most influential saints had a rough start: Paul the Apostle made it his personal business to persecute Christians before his conversion; Saint Augustine was a partying, drunken, womanizer before his; Dorothy Day was a Communist who had an abortion; Mary Magdalene was a "woman of ill repute." We all have people in our lives who have taken wrong turns (maybe we have), whom we hope and pray will know the truth about their worth to us and to God. These stories give us hope for them, too.

Throughout the movie *X Men: Days of Future Past*, Professor Xavier repeats a sentiment about his hope for the mutants who are causing trouble in the world. He says, "Just because someone stumbles and loses their way, doesn't mean that they are lost forever." He knew the wayward mutants before they were wayward. He knows there's good in them. It's just like our love for the broken, and even more so, God's love for us. We remember and we hope.

Many of Jesus's stories of redemption are the result of an individual seeking it: Zacchaeus, Mary Magdalene, the Syrophoenician woman, the good thief on the cross. Many others were invited to redemption when they were in the thick of their sin. The woman caught in adultery was dragged into the street (her lover nowhere to be found—probably wearing a towel with rock in hand) and about to be killed by the men of the town. As she is naked, ashamed, afraid, and no doubt hopeless, Jesus becomes help unlooked for. He's not judgmental, but gently exposes the unfair judgment of the men in the town. He reminds them that, unless they're sinless, they need to put their rocks down. When Jesus has saved the woman's life and they're alone, their conversation is loving and compassionate. He stands up straight to look her in the eye as he addresses her, saying, "'Woman, where are they? Has no one condemned you?' She said, 'No one, sir.' And Jesus said, 'Neither do I condemn you. Go your way, and from now on do not sin again'" (John 8:10–11). That's it. He sees her brokenness; he sees who she truly is, not her sin. He calls her "woman," a title of honor, the same title he calls his mother. He treats her with dignity and respect—which she may have never experienced in her life. He frees her from guilt and charges her to be who he knows she can be. He restores her hope.

When speaking of Mystique, Professor X says, "I cannot believe that is who she is." He means he can't believe that she's a baddie. He knew her as a vulnerable, lost child. He knew her as a young woman trying to find her way. He knows that she and the other mutants do seek justice, but they're going about it the wrong way. He knows that she wants good, but is confused about how to find it. At the end of the movie, Wolverine asks, "You sure you should let them go?" Professor X says, "Yes. I have hope for them. There's going to be a time when we are one together." His words sound like the words of a loving father. Our loving Father says the same thing.

Consider the story of the prodigal son. The younger son takes the inheritance that he feels is owed him—while his father is alive—and leaves his family as if they were dead. He spends the money on morally corrupt living until he finds himself completely out of resources. He decides to go home and ask forgiveness—for no other reason than that his stomach was empty. We see in this story that the father was outside scanning the horizon in hope that his boy would come home: "But while he was still far off, his father saw him and was filled with compassion; he ran and put his arms around him and kissed him" (Luke 15:20). He greets him, forgives him, and restores him perfectly in status, authority, and wealth, and even throws a party for him. When Jesus tells us of the father's hope being fulfilled in having his son return, it's meant to illustrate God's hope in each of his children—regardless of what evil they have done—to come home again and be restored.

It's God's desire that everyone be reconciled and choose to be with him forever in heaven. He lets us go on our own path, always inviting us to walk with him, always hoping that we'll accept his help to find true peace. Who knows what effect Xavier's hope and his consistent invitation will have on Magneto and Mystique and the crew? We see that they can work together in this movie and in *X-Men: Apocalypse*; we know that they have a common purpose. Like Xavier, we hope for their reconciliation.

Reconciliation

This is what the sacrament of reconciliation is all about. It's God's invitation to see ourselves as we truly are, and as we're meant to be. It's an opportunity to choose hope instead of despair. It's an opportunity to realize that we're better together than apart. Jesus sacrificed himself so that we could know how much he loves us, and the sacrament of reconciliation is where we embrace that love and let it redirect and guide our lives. It's where we abandon the things we never wanted to be, and become what we have always deep down believed that we could be.

God wants so much for us to be reconciled that he made it his mission to come here to show us personally what that meant. It wasn't the "Don't make me come over there!" that parents say to their misbehaving kids. It was total self-giving, self-emptying love, so that we could know what it feels like to be filled. Sin makes us feel empty. God created us to be fulfilled. Like Batman, Luke Skywalker, and Professor X, we're given the same ministry of reconciliation that Jesus took upon himself. Each of us has been on the wrong side of things and has needed forgiveness. And, no doubt, each of us has experienced forgiveness. Since we have been recipients, it's up to us to help the other broken people in the world to know that it's available to them, too.

Forgiving others is a matter of justice. If we can't extend to others—or if we deliberately withhold from others—what has been freely given to us, we risk becoming corrupt. We must recognize that we're always one bad choice away from disaster ourselves. You know that phrase, "There but for the grace of God go I"? It's true. It's only by God's grace and our willingness to accept and share it that we don't descend into darkness ourselves. If we choose to hold onto our anger, embrace our hate, reciprocate pain to those who hurt us, we risk becoming villains ourselves. We become unjust judges, believing that we're entitled to meet out punishment for our wounds. That's what villains do.

The prodigal son had a brother. You wouldn't really consider *him* a villain because he stayed home and dutifully cared for his worried, bereft parents while continuing his work as he always did. He's responsible. He's a *good* son...until his brother comes home. Apparently, the whole time his younger brother was gone, the brother was harboring resentments (which most people would be able to identify with and probably even agree with). He resented his brother for leaving, his father for never acknowledging his steadfastness, maybe even himself for not speaking up. When he discovered that his brother was home and that there was a party going on to celebrate his return, and that *he wasn't even invited* (okay, I'd be mad, too), he refuses to even go in. He doesn't want to forgive his brother, and he doesn't want to forgive his father for restoring his brother. He's only concerned with the injustice that he perceives was done to him. Think about that for a second: he considers his father's forgiveness toward his brother an injustice to *him*. He judges everyone else in the story and justifies his own uncharity. Probably every reader will say, "Well, I've done *that*," and I have, too. It's natural to feel that way for a time. But we're given the sense that maybe he stubbornly held onto that anger and might not have even gone inside due to what he experienced as wounded pride. He may have chosen to cultivate his anger rather than enter heaven (the party). He's on a good road toward villainy.

When I remember who I am and what mission God has given to me, I can be hope to someone who might be teetering on the edge of supervillainy. I must challenge my own pain and self-doubt, trust that God is faithful even when I'm not, and have hope in forgiveness and peace. I must live that hope as justice in every situation I'm faced with; that has the potential to bring healing. This is what heroes do.

CHAPTER SEVEN

BATMAN

Wounded Healer

A Light in the Darkness

We all know Batman's backstory (unless you live in a cave, although living in a cave might improve your chances of knowing about Batman). Bruce was a tween when his incredibly wealthy parents were mugged (a mob hit) and gunned down in a dark alley right in front of him, leaving him the richest orphan in Gotham, in the care of the family butler. That alone would be a more than acceptable backstory for a villain. No one would blame Bruce if he, with every earthly advantage, became a spoiled, entitled brat bent on hurting anyone who came in his path to assuage the pain of losing his parents at such a young age and the feelings of guilt and shame that would have accompanied his survival of the attack. But this is not the backstory of a villain. It's the backstory of one of the greatest heroes ever. EVER.

Bruce's caregiver, Alfred Pennyworth, was not just a butler. He cared deeply for Bruce and for Bruce's parents, Martha and Thomas. He was also an intelligence agent for the British armed forces, which made him a perfect assistant to Batman later. His early guidance and intentional reinforcement of the values that Martha and Thomas Wayne worked hard to instill in their son very likely prevented Bruce from becoming one of the villains he would later suppress. Alfred taught Bruce to believe in justice (as did Jim Gordon, the police officer who would become commissioner), and that Bruce's unique, inherited position and resources meant that he had great responsibility to be a force for good—particularly for the poor and marginalized.

Bruce has a very dark story. His heart never really mended from the loss of his parents. He felt fearful, alone, broken, and angry. Like anyone seeking healing and personal discovery, Bruce had to do a lot of work to become a contributing member of society and to live up to his responsibilities. He wanted justice for his parents, and his heart was restless as he sought it. As a young man needing to find himself, as many young people do, he went on a journey that was as much spiritual as it was physical. Bruce found a martial arts master with whom he studied relentlessly until he became proficient at those arts, enabling him to blend into the shadows of Gotham or anywhere else he chose to be.

He spent his life looking for inner peace as a salve for the pain of losing his parents in that terrible way. He was also looking for justice, and felt that if he pursued justice for his parents (and Gotham), he would find the peace he sought. But he remained unsettled in his spirit; he remained wounded and incomplete. However, unlike many people, Bruce didn't use his woundedness as an excuse to hurt others. Using his acquired skills, he became something of a detective, and his method of discovering the truth didn't include inflicting unnecessary harm on anyone—not even bad guys.

As Batman, Bruce operated within the shadows—he entered the darkness of the ugly places in Gotham to root out the darkness of crime. In many ways, darkness was part of him—he suffered a lot and, he's often shown as rather broody (especially Will Arnett's perfect portrayal in the *Lego Batman Movie*). But in most incarnations, he doesn't let the darkness become him. Let's explore these themes.

There's a parallel with Christ here. Jesus entered the darkness of our world to root out evil and sin. As mentioned earlier, John's Gospel says that "the light shines in the darkness, and the darkness did not overcome it" (John 1:5). Batman stepped into the shadows night after night, looking for evil so he could root it out, but he never allowed the endlessness of his mission to corrupt his heart. That's saying a lot. Parish ministry has been ruining perfectly nice, well-intentioned people for as long as there have been parish offices. Dealing with the rudeness, lying, cheating, and stealing that comes with working with regular people—not even *super*villains—day in and day out has broken many a parish secretary. But Batman deals with the worst of the worst, and manages to keep his focus.

I've often wondered if Bruce Wayne wasn't Jesuit educated. He's brilliant, compassionate, has a great sense of justice, and seems to have a very Ignatian understanding of personal freedom. Even when he faces, after decades of searching, his parents' killer, Bruce proves that the darkness hasn't overcome him.

In the animated series *Batman: The Brave and The Bold*, there's an episode, "Chill of the Night," in which Bruce finally does meet the man who killed his parents, Joe Chill. In the episode, Batman confronts Joe and reveals his identity to him. That's a bold move, because as we know, Batman never kills anyone, and now there's a guy who knows he's Bruce Wayne. Joe, not trusting his future to Batman's past values, realizes his peril, and attacks Batman, who responds in kind...with *maybe* a *little* extra. Okay, a *lot* extra. But when Batman has subdued Joe, two opposing forces appear to Batman offering possible outcomes to the situation. His better angel says, "He is beaten. Let your devotion to justice temper your rage." The other reminds him of the suffering he's experienced all these years, what was taken from him, and that the man knows who he is. This voice tells him to "become what you have trained to be; an agent of vengeance." The voice says, "If this man lives, Batman dies."

Bruce knows himself. He's able to act in serious personal freedom because he's been pursuing it his whole career. He never advanced his own freedom by taking another's, and so, because of these years of practice, responds in freedom even in the most emotionally charged situation. He responds, "Batman may die, but Bruce Wayne...never." He's not willing to compromise his integrity, the core of his being, to protect his alter ego. If he killed Joe Chill, the Batman that he had been all those years would cease to exist.

He was willing to allow a part of himself to die in favor of preserving the most important part of him. To me, Batman is like a living Sermon on the Mount. The justice he seeks is a Beatitude for Gotham. In the moment he meets the murderer of his parents, he refuses to hide his light under a bushel basket, or to allow his saltiness to lose its flavor. He is all about upholding the law, doesn't retain anger against his enemy when faced with it, and would rather cut off one of his limbs than allow his true self (I'd say "soul") to be lost.

In Christianity, we share such a concept. In the Gospel of Luke, Jesus says, "If any want to become my followers, let them deny themselves and take up their cross daily and follow me. For those who want to save their life will lose it, and those who lose their life for my sake will save it" (Luke 9:23-24). Like Batman, or like Jesus, if we want to live in the true freedom of the children of God, we must be willing to sacrifice the parts of us that would prevent us from living justice. And, just like Batman...or Jesus... when we are willing to sacrifice such things, we effectively lose nothing. In his willingness to give up his secret identity, Batman retained his anonymity, allowing him to continue his fight for justice. In his willingness to die on the cross, Jesus gained resurrection for himself and eternal life for us. If we are willing to give up parents, or houses, or children, or whatever, Jesus promises us, "There is no one who has left house or brothers or sisters or mother or father or children or fields, for my sake and for the sake of the good news, who will not receive a hundredfold now in this age—houses, brothers and sisters, mothers and children, and fields, with persecutions—and in the age to come eternal life" (Mark 10:29-30). We get back everything we gave up one hundredfold—plus persecutions! Tell me *that's* not a sweet deal. More opportunities to practice justice!

Back to the cartoon episode: not only did Batman not kill Joe, but he tried to save Joe's life when Joker and almost the whole Rogue's Gallery came along a little later and tried to kill him. In true villain form, when they discover that Joe's murder of Bruce's parents is what caused him to become Batman, constantly thwarting their plans, they turn on Joe. He begs them for help in the spirit of their being colleagues and on the same side, but when you engage in evil, no one is on your side. Everyone ultimately looks out for their own interests. He finds no help with them, and ironically, fled from the one person who would have brought him to justice and kept him safe, because good ultimately looks out for the best interest of others.

Wounded Healers

Batman knew that most of the villains he was dealing with were criminally insane and, therefore, not acting with much personal freedom. So he acted with restraint and compassion toward the villains—it makes me think of Saint Ignatius's teaching on personal freedom. The more we're in union with God, the freer our actions become—not irresponsible or libertarian, but intentional and deliberate. Instead of losing ourselves by reacting blindly out of frustration, pain, and anger, our character remains intact when we carefully consider and choose our responses. This kind of freedom comes with much prayer and reflection—it comes with peace of heart and an understanding of what motivates us. It also comes with an understanding of other people's personal freedom—or lack thereof.

Criminally insane people are incapable of making good decisions. Criminally insane people don't have enough command of themselves to be very free. And people who have been beaten down and then thrown into a circus sideshow because they look like a crocodile probably never had the luxury of learning how to treat people with dignity and kindness. So, when Batman meets a guy like Killer Croc, he knows he must stop his violent, homicidal rampage, but he doesn't judge him. He tries to help him. He offers him the opportunity to change.

Again, I see Jesus's reflection here. Jesus, being both divine and human, had perfect understanding of the human condition.

He was our Creator, and he was one of us. So, when he encountered wounded people who were acting out of their pain, confusion, or ignorance, he made it his business to give them another option. Matthew tells us, "When [Jesus] saw the crowds, he had compassion for them, because they were harassed and helpless, like sheep without a shepherd" (Matt 9:36). They hadn't been given what they needed to claim full agency for their lives. And that's what Jesus is all about. He wants us to be able to freely accept the gift of love that God offers us. But we need to know how. As Philip was convicted by his encounter with the Ethiopian eunuch, "How can I, unless someone guides me?" (Acts 8:31). How can anyone know what's right unless they're taught?

Batman's way of "guiding" villains was to give them an experience of justice. If he could treat them with dignity and try to get them help in Arkham, or to get them rehabilitated in the most excellent correctional facilities of Gotham (well, maybe not), they might see the error of their ways and make better choices if they ever were paroled...or broke out. But even before he turned many of them over to the police, he tried to help them.

Clayface was originally an actor, Matt Hagen, who was in a terrible accident. While attempting to reconstruct his face, a doctor made him a test subject for a new chemical compound that would make his face malleable. It didn't go as planned and needed to be reapplied a lot for his face to retain its shape. He grew addicted to it, and eventually, it made his whole body malleable. He had the ability to take any shape, but when he wasn't making himself look like someone, he looked like a scary, brown blob. To make things worse, the doctor would only give him the compound if Matt took on the appearance of others and engaged in illegal activities for the doctor's gain. All these unfortunate circumstances shaped him into a supervillain.

By the time Batman got to him (well, he got to Batman), he was losing control of his ability to take and keep a shape. After Clayface mocked and tried to kill him, Batman begged him to let him try and help him. He showed Clayface pictures of the various roles he had played in his career. "Look at them, Hagen. Look at what you used to be. You can play those roles again, Hagen. Let me help you find a cure." It was too late for Clayface—he was so far gone from using the stuff that he became any image he looked at. The images of what he used to be overwhelmed him as he morphed out of control.

Batman's mercy toward Clayface might have come from his own experience. He was playing a part by being Batman, and amid the mockery and attempted murder he encountered with Clayface and every other villain he met, he would have to remind himself of who he really was. He had to fight to retain himself, his personal freedom, rather than to give in to the fear, stress, or anger of what he was facing. His plea to Clayface is heartfelt—it's not just a moral obligation, it's a desire to help an otherwise decent man regain his footing so he can reclaim his life. He wants to stop the man's suffering because he knows what it is to feel lost. Batman knows how easily a body could get off track when the choices look so limited.

The story of Batman and Clayface isn't unique to the tales of Batman. I think his compassion was partially grown through his own suffering. We're all meant to be wounded healers—not that God desires our pain, but that God changes our pain (when we let him) into empathy. It's clear that Batman wasn't cured of his wounded heart—the darkness is where he's comfortable because that's what he knows. Just as our role as wounded healer doesn't mean that our wounds are taken away from us, it also doesn't mean that we should try to remain in pain. To be a healer, one must have experienced healing in oneself. Consider the Twelve Step Programs. Recovering addicts are the most help to addicts because they can see healing in action. Any addict will tell you that they're never "cured" of their addiction, but learn to live with it one day at a time. We aren't meant to remain in the throes of our suffering or grief, but are meant to allow them to be transformed, and allow ourselves to be transformed, so that we can be strong enough to let God carry us through one day at a time.

This is why bereavement support groups work. If I've never suffered significant loss in my life, I can tell you about the stages of grief theoretically, but that's not the same as one who has walked that road and can tell you from lived experience what to expect. Those who have suffered bereavement know what the newly bereft need. I may sympathize, but one who has lost can empathize. But if one has suffered a loss that they haven't learned to cope with, they won't be helpful to anyone. People who remain stuck—not seeking healing, but remaining in the same place as when the loss was fresh—drag others down with them. To be a wounded healer, you must be making an authentic attempt to be healed and have found some success. To be a wounded healer, you must be involved in getting at the heart of the matter—not just the symptoms.

Batman is partially driven by his pain, driven by his anger at the injustice of being robbed of his parents so young and so terribly. Being driven to bring their killer to justice puts him in the path of countless villains that he thwarts along the way. But he's not out to put a Band-Aid on the problem of crime by rounding up petty thieves. He wants to strike at the heart of the disease, the corruption, which for believers is a stand-in for sin.

Gotham is a rough city, and the villains aren't the only ones causing trouble. The Gotham Police are horrendously corrupt, which exacerbates the problem. Batman works behind the scenes to stop crime, in part, because the cops and some higher-ups are on the take, and a lot of good, honest policework is undone by payoffs and bribes. Batman becomes a stumbling block for anyone who opposes justice with his honesty and integrity. The corrupt in Gotham call him a "vigilante"; some say he's a menace, and his methods certainly don't fit into their style of crime-fighting, which is only keeping the status quo.

Jesus did the same. He didn't fit the norm of the rabbis of his day. His methods were unorthodox—he healed on the Sabbath, hung out with the wrong people, didn't fast the way a lot of preacher/healers did. For some, his methods were a stumbling block. He also didn't accept the status quo, and was not keen on allowing the crimes against the poor and marginalized to go unchallenged: "'The stone that the builders rejected / has become the very head of the corner,' / and / 'A stone that makes them stumble, / and a rock that makes them fall.' They stumble because they disobey the word, as they were destined to do" (1 Pet 2:7–8).

The cornerstone is not rectangular like other building blocks. It's a kind of wedge that holds up the whole arch and strengthens the structure around it. When looking for building materials, it could easily be tossed aside because it doesn't match the criteria for general building—it's a specialized piece. Batman is a bit misshapen for typical crime fighting because he doesn't look like a cop, follow the rules of the cops, and is only vaguely associated with the cops through his relationship with

Commissioner Gordon. He's also misshapen because his heart needs repair. His brokenness doesn't make him a less effective crime fighter; it makes him more compassionate and hell-bent for justice. He can't be bought and he can't be distracted from his mission. He's seeking his own healing as he seeks the healing of each criminal, the wider Gotham, and then the universe when he gets hooked up with the Justice League.

His efforts (together with Robin, Batgirl, and the Justice League) infuse strength into the corrupt justice system of Gotham. The justice and mercy with which he treats the Rogues automatically make the system better, even if the other players don't play along. He makes a difference by pursuing justice and embodying it on the streets. He brings hope to the citizens of Gotham, to the good police officers, at times even to the villains themselves. He helps Commissioner Gordon be better at his job and makes Gotham safer.

Jesus didn't overthrow the Romans. He didn't incite protests against the rulers at all. He didn't take his rightful place as King of the Universe in that time and place and make the religious or civil leaders do their jobs properly. He brought mercy, healing, love, forgiveness, and true understanding of God and what it meant to be a good Jew. Jesus's actions made Israel better because they gave hope to the citizens who had encounters with him. He enabled people to change their lives and make more life-giving decisions, finding more personal freedom the more they knew him.

A Ministry of Reconciliation

You might not immediately associate Batman with "gentleness," but that's one of the qualities I most love in him. He doesn't kill. He usually doesn't even use more force than is used against him with his enemies. He uses finesse. Being a master of martial arts, self-control and discipline are second nature to him. He can do much with little, but skilled, effort. He can disable a person and prevent them from causing further harm without harming them any more than he must. In *Batman: The Animated Series*, his "victims" were most often left with bruised egos and broken plans more than physical ailments. They would just be hanging or sitting, tied up and waiting for the police to come and take them safely into custody.

What I'm calling "gentleness" here is really Batman's hope of reconciliation. Scripture tells us that God wouldn't bother correcting us if he didn't consider us worth being reconciled with. I don't think Batman would bother taking so much care with the villains if he didn't think they were worth trying to rehabilitate and reconcile. He may have taken so much care with them for the sake of his own reconciliation, too.

Like all wounded healers, we're interested in preventing or curing what ails others, but we also seek redemption for ourselves. We want to know that what has hurt us can be overcome, so we find proof of it in those we serve. It's like an old woman who was unlucky in love becoming a yenta. She wants to believe that true love is a real thing (maybe she watched *The Princess Bride* too many times), and tries to help other people find it, certainly to bring them joy and maybe restore her faith in love, too.

In fact, we all have a mission to build one another up. God made us in God's own image and likeness, and God built us for community. Our being made in God's image means that personal freedom is a real thing, true love is a real thing, and our mission is to find them and live them out. This can happen when we remember who we truly are (like Batman tried to help Clayface do) by virtue of our baptism, and we do the hard work of being reconciled where we've strayed from being the image of God.

As Saint Paul says, "All this is from God, who reconciled us to himself through Christ, and has given us the ministry of reconciliation; that is, in Christ God was reconciling the world to himself, not counting their trespasses against them, and entrusting the message of reconciliation to us. So we are ambassadors for Christ, since God is making his appeal through us; we entreat you on behalf of Christ, be reconciled to God" (2 Cor 5:18–20). This is what I think Batman is trying to do (in less theological terms) when he corrects the Rogues.

We're not supposed to allow people to persist in sin without giving them an option for another way, but we must do it with a sincere and loving heart, with the recognition that we're at least as bad off as they are. Batman doesn't catch the bad guys and then tell them how awful they are. He either tries to help them, like he did Clayface, or he says nothing while they berate him.

In the last chapter, I briefly mentioned Zacchaeus. He was a tax collector who cheated people, partly because it was his job and partly because he was a greedy little man. Tax collectors were assessed an amount that they had to hand over to the Romans—and they got it however they could. If Biff and Buffy down the street didn't have what they owed, he'd take extra from Hans and Brunhild. And then he'd take extra wherever he could so he could make a commission. Zacchaeus sinned against the law of God by stealing, and against his countrymen by collecting taxes for their occupiers, and he needs correction. How does Jesus deal with this guy? He invites himself over to dinner.

Their conversation is interesting. Honestly, the whole conversation was Jesus saying, "Zacchaeus, hurry and come down; for I must stay at your house today" (Luke 19:5). The "correction" Jesus offered was nothing more than his presence. Kindness. Attention. Jesus invited Zacchaeus to be reconciled just by having dinner with him. It was probably the first time anyone was nice to him. Zacchaeus's response, presumably without Jesus even suggesting it, was to give half of his possessions to the poor, and "if" he cheated anyone, to give back four times the worth of it. His short time with Jesus was life changing. How do we know it was life changing? Because Zacchaeus immediately sought to reconcile his actions to the people he hurt.

Most of us aren't having dinner with tax collectors and prostitutes. When we're dealing with the very ordinary brokenness of others, it's far less cut-and-dried. And in our "don't judge me" society, it's even more challenging. We have the idea that pointing out a wrong or noticing a destructive behavior is judgmental. Of course, one can make a correction without making a judgment—and that's what's expected of Christians. We aren't supposed to see people being hurt, treated unjustly, or heading for trouble and remain silent. We're supposed to lovingly offer another way. If we pretend not to see a problem, we're complicit in it.

Ezekiel was told by God that if he didn't deliver the warning messages to Israel, that he'd be responsible for their sin. If "you do not speak to warn the wicked to turn from their ways, the wicked shall die in their iniquity, but their blood I will require at your hand. But if you warn the wicked to turn from their ways, and they do not turn from their ways, the wicked shall die in their iniquity, but you will have saved your life" (Ezek 33:8–9). As responsible as we are to forgive people and not judge them, we're equally responsible for letting them know if they're headed for danger. Or, if someone has hurt you and you keep telling them everything is "fine," they don't have the opportunity to apologize and be forgiven. You continue to bear a grudge, which we're also not supposed to do, and it makes you bitter and corrupts your heart and relationships.

So Batman can offer us yet another useful life hack: address evil head-on. When he became aware of a plot, or a villain that needed stopping, or some corruption that needed a light shone on it, he went right for it. If we pussyfoot around evil, we give evil more room to grow and more opportunity to catch us in sin. If we pretend not to see it, we participate in it by our sin of omission. If we prefer to keep our resentments rather than address our hurts, we and our offenders remain stuck. But if we call evil what it is, we can put our feelings in their proper place, put injustice in its proper place, and begin to address our hurts, taking away their power to keep us stuck. Part of being a wounded healer is taking steps in any situation to effectively bring healing, not pretend it's not needed.

Being honest about our feelings and sharing our struggles with others is personally a little risky because it requires us to leave the safety of the shadows and to bring our feelings or bad situations into the light. We don't know how people will respond to us. We risk rejection, labeling, judgment—all things that feel very much like the opposite of reconciliation. But sometimes we need to get through that stuff to get to the good stuff. We should try very hard not to be afraid, because whether it's us or someone else who brings it up, all evil will eventually come to light anyway. Jesus said, "So have no fear of them; for nothing is covered up that will not be uncovered, and nothing secret that will not become known" (Matt 10:26). People weren't always fond of Batman when he did his crime fighting, but he kept at it because he knew it was right and he wanted to facilitate as much healing in Gotham and in his own heart as he could. He put the needs of the community above his own comfort, just like Jesus asks us to do.

CHAPTER EIGHT

WIZARDS

God's Not a Magician

True Freedom of the Children of God

Wizards like Gandalf and Dumbledore can conjure up almost anything and could probably just erase all our problems with magic. But they don't. They offer help (sometimes even butt in) and at times sacrifice themselves for the cause, but they don't use magic as an easy fix. When we're amid suffering, we say the same about God—why doesn't God just fix it?

Questioning the motives or actions of heroes and villains—or even God—is natural. We watch and yell, "Why didn't he just...," or, "What was she thinking when...," or, "The whole thing would be over if he would just...," and solutions that seem completely obvious to any couch-writer at home keep our heroes mystified. Then there are the characters who we think could fix any problem, but don't seem to use their full power to defeat evil.

One example that pops up is Gandalf from *The Hobbit* and *The Lord of the Rings*. Since Gandalf is a wizard, he knows magic and has power that's far beyond most of the other characters he works with. He's not all-powerful, but he's powerful enough to destroy a Balrog, an ancient, demonic fire-beast of terrible power (he dies defeating the Balrog, but returns stronger than before). When you ponder Gandalf's magic and his abilities to speak to insects and animals, cast and remove spells, harness light, and fight, one might have the impression that Gandalf could have done far more than he did throughout the stories.

Sometimes this same thought occurs to people about God. A favorite argument of atheists about whether there is a God, or how we can think our God is good, is the question of why, if the God we believe in *is* good, does God allow evil in the world. They see evil in the world as evidence against God. When we look at evils—especially ones that involve the most innocent and vulnerable people—it's natural to ask, "How can a loving, just God allow things like this to happen?" The answers to this question are as varied as the people who answer; "God has a plan," "God only gives what we can handle," "God is punishing us," or even things as blasphemous as "God hates *them*." We need an answer, because it's a good question. If I have a child, I'm going to do whatever I can to preserve that child from danger and pain. But, unlike God, I'm *not* all-powerful, so of course I'll fail. God *is* all-powerful, so how can God, who claims to love us, fail? Like with the movies we watch and the books we read, we're tempted to say, "Why doesn't he just...," or ,"What was he thinking when...," or, "The whole thing would be over if...." Couldn't God do more? Shouldn't God? It's an ancient question.

But here's the rub; God made us for love. True love can't be required—only requited. An unfortunate byproduct of this is suffering because some people just aren't going to accept the love that's offered to them. In the Book of Genesis, chapter 1, right after humanity was created, we were given a couple of jobs: be fruitful and multiply, and have dominion over the Earth. In chapter 2, we were also given a restriction: don't eat the fruit of the Tree of the Knowledge of Good and Evil. And so, we ask, why on earth, if God didn't want us to do something, would he stick that *very* thing in the dead center of the garden? Isn't that just setting us up for failure? Isn't that a little mean? It's like those people who put a dog treat on their puppy's nose and say, "Stay," right?

To answer these perfectly legitimate questions, we must deconstruct the story a little. The story of the fall of humanity isn't about an apple (it *never once* mentions an apple), a talking snake, a nudist colony, or fig leaves for clothes. It's a representation of our being made in God's image and likeness, with the power of reason, understanding, intellect, the capacity for love, and our freedom to use them. Or not. For us to be made in God's image and likeness, we must be free. To experience love, and to share it, we must be free. To be free, a choice must be present.

When you think about it, the only ones in our hero stories who try to force their will on others, and who try to *make* people love them, are villains. They don't believe in truth, justice, and the American way, and they don't believe that anyone should be allowed to oppose them. It's heroes who preserve our right to make choices and to fail royally. And God does too. The story of the fall of humanity is the story of how God loved us so much that he let us not choose him. That's what love does: love gives you the freedom to not choose it.

Just as there are no magic spells or formulas God uses to make us do what he wants, we don't cast spells to influence others or God. There can be a temptation, especially among the faithful in the Catholic Church, to think that if we use the right words or follow the right formula, we can make God do what we want. Because we often use formulaic prayer, some Catholics feel they haven't prayed correctly when they've asked God for something but didn't get it. We sometimes forget that God, too, has free will and isn't made in our image, and isn't our puppet any more than we are his. No formula will cause God to give us what we shouldn't have, nor will God violate the will of any of his other creatures for our gain. When we pray for others to change or heal (or whatever), God may help them to become more open to the gifts that God offers, or to see them more clearly for what they are, but God will never force anyone to change. The purpose of prayer is to change the pray-er, not to use magic spells to impose our will on others. This is outside the design of a loving being, and so has no place in our relationship with God.

God made us out of love with the intention that we'd live in love and, therefore, be happy. In the Gospel of John, Jesus says, "As the Father has loved me, so I have loved you; abide in my love. If you keep my commandments, you will abide in my love, just as I have kept my Father's commandments and abide in his love. I have said these things to you so that my joy may be in you, and that your joy may be complete" (John 15:9–11). The result of accepting and responding to God's love is joy, and that could only be if it was chosen.

Lord of the Rings Lessons

Incidents in *The Fellowship of the Ring*, when the Fellowship is in Lothlórien, remind me of this very passage. Celeborn and Galadriel, the Elven Lord and Lady of Lothlórien, were extremely wise, powerful, and magical. They weren't thrilled that the Ring was in their kingdom, because they knew the evil it brought with it, but they welcomed the Fellowship and offered them hospitality. When the Elves were first hearing their story, Galadriel searched the hearts of the company. Each felt that she had offered (telepathically) an easy way out of their quest, which would give them their heart's desire and remain secret. Each of them felt that it was a test to see if they could fulfill what they had started.

The "commandment," if you will, was the task they all accepted to help Frodo get to Mount Doom to cast the Ring into the fire. If they hadn't kept it, the proper outcome wouldn't have occurred, and getting their heart's desire would have been only a pipe dream, because evil Sauron's conquest would have succeeded and they would have become slaves. Galadriel knew that the Ring would only be destroyed if everyone played their proper part. They couldn't be forced to do what needed to be done; they each had to freely choose it. Only when the quest had been completed would their own joy be complete.

Later, Galadriel and Frodo, as the time for the Fellowship to move on was approaching, spoke together about the future of the Elves in Middle-earth. Their time of dominance in Middle-earth was up, and they were making their way into the West to "diminish." The time of Men was coming. Galadriel knew that the Ring showing up in Lothlórien was a sign that their time was very short. Frodo offered her the Ring, thinking that this was the solution to his problem and hers. After all, she was wise and good—maybe she could hold onto the Ring and everything would be fine. Galadriel knew that, though it was tempting, that wasn't a power she was interested in wielding—in her words, if she took it, "All shall love me and despair!"

Even one who is very good like Galadriel, if given the power of enforcing obedience, would become a tyrant. As she was, Galadriel was a leader of the fairest people in Middle-earth—she was respected and revered by the Elves and by all who met her. People who encountered her experienced a deeper level of freedom because they understood that they had choices. If she had accepted the power of the Ring, the "love" they would have for her would only reap despair; first because of the loss of herself to the lust that the Ring produces, and second because it would ultimately have been a victory for Sauron. Even Galadriel had a part to play in the quest—to be a giver of hospitality and gifts that aided the Fellowship immensely, and to remain herself: to "diminish, and go into the West, and remain Galadriel."

God gave us hearts in freedom so that we could live in the true love that is freely offered, freely received, and makes us more ourselves when we embrace it. That passage in John's Gospel continues,

> This is my commandment, that you love one another as I have loved you. No one has greater love than this, to lay down one's life for one's friends. You are my friends if you do what I command you. I do not call you servants any longer, because the servant does not know what the master is doing; but I have called you friends, because I have made known to you everything that I have heard from my Father. You did not choose me but I chose you. And I appointed you to go and bear fruit, fruit that will last, so that the Father will give you whatever you ask him in my name. I am giving you these commands so that you may love one another. (John 15:12–17)

When God chose us as recipients of his love, he offered us everything that he had. God calls us friends, and wants us to be willing participants in his love. The commandment to love one another the way that Jesus loves us can only be carried out in personal freedom. Jesus, though he asked to be spared, chose to die for us because of his love for the Father and for us. His obedience was in perfect freedom so that we could learn from him and follow in his footsteps. He's not asking us to do anything that he wasn't willing to do first, and what he's asking—not demanding—is that we make sacrifices for the good of others. It does not benefit God when we do—God neither gains nor loses anything from our actions—but when we follow God's commandments, the world benefits.

God's a Hopeless Romantic

Personal freedom is super important to God. Wanting creatures who could love him back, God made us little so that we could grow. God made us ignorant so we could learn. God made us creative and loving so we could share in God's activity. God wanted to make creatures who would have genius, and let that genius shine. For that to happen, God had to give us a certain amount of autonomy. God would tell us how to go about achieving greatness, but would have to allow us to make our way to it and through it by striking out on our own—not without help—but with the freedom to make choices, for better or for worse.

I see this theme reflected in *The Lord of the Rings*. As the time approached for Aragorn to take his place on the throne of Gondor, he still had some growing to do. Battles needed to be fought and won, armies needed to be led, kingly attributes that were natural to Aragorn needed to be developed and strengthened for him to become what he needed to be for the people of Middle-earth. If Gandalf had just blown through and defeated the bad guys, if he had imposed his will instead of helping people like Aragorn, Faramir, Éowyn, the Hobbits, and Théoden grow into greatness, Gandalf would have had to remain in Middle-earth to keep things running properly. The leadership that emerged through the struggles of making Middle-earth safe and bringing the various peoples together wouldn't have been established if magic made it easy. They wouldn't have reached their potential and wouldn't have been prepared if any other obstacles came their way.

The Fellowship spoke repeatedly of Gandalf as their "guide." They knew he was powerful. Maybe they didn't know quite how powerful he was, but they didn't expect him to solve everything. That's not a guide's job. A guide provides information, direction, support, and help to avoid danger and disaster, but does not fight your battles for you or drag you along the path. One of the most important moments with Gandalf in the company of the Fellowship was a small conversation he shared with Frodo. In the very beginning of Frodo's journey, he laments that his uncle, Bilbo, didn't kill Gollum when he had the chance—when Gollum was vulnerable. He said it was a "pity" that Bilbo didn't kill him. Gandalf responded that, "It was pity that stayed his hand...." This pity or mercy believes that Gollum can change. It hopes that there's still some good in there, but even if there isn't, it believes that protecting the brokenness in Gollum is a worthy pursuit. Gollum never became good. The Ring had wounded him so deeply that he was never able to recover and be freed from its pull.

But the image of pity or mercy and the value of living things (even when they're repulsive like Gollum) that Gandalf offered

Frodo took root in him. Frodo could go back to that image and advocate for Gollum even when there was very little reason to do so. It seemed to backfire on him, because although Gollum got Frodo and Sam very far in their journey, he betrayed them and tried to get Frodo killed by Shelob, the enormous man- (and Orc-) eating spider, so that he'd have another opportunity to grab The Ring. Ultimately, Frodo's sparing of Gollum was the only thing that made their quest successful. If Gollum hadn't attacked Frodo when he was standing at the precipice of Mount Doom, Frodo never would have parted with The Ring, and Sauron would have taken over Middle-earth. Gandalf's compassion, imparted to Frodo and wasted on Gollum, saved the world.

We see a similar relationship between wizards and wizards-in-training in the Harry Potter series. The professors at Hogwarts taught the young wizards what they would need to know so that they could fulfill their potential. It didn't mean removing all the obstacles they would encounter. It meant accompanying the young ones through them, offering protection against creatures or enemies that were too powerful for them, or helping to unpack the experiences when they were over, because sometimes the adventures that the young wizards had were meant only for them.

Sometimes theologians talk about the Holy Spirit as God's action on Earth. Jesus talks about the Holy Spirit as Paraclete, a guide or counselor. God's not using mind control or zapping us every time we get out of line. God isn't a friend of karma, making us pay for our evil deeds, but instead, "He makes his sun rise on the evil and on the good, and sends rain on the righteous and on the unrighteous" (Matt 5:45). God offers us truth about what will be sources of joy for us and what will be sources of pain, and then lets us make our own decisions about how we're going to live—always with an open heart to take comfort and forgive us when we choose wrong.

You see, God's a hopeless romantic. God knows that love will always prevail. God hopes beyond hope that when we're given the freedom to choose love, we will. In Jesus's parable of the wheat and weeds, he likens God to a farmer who was trying to grow wheat. An enemy came and scattered the seeds of weeds among his wheat, hoping to ruin the harvest. The farmer (God) lets the wheat and weeds grow up together because "in gathering the weeds you would uproot the wheat along with them. Let both of them grow together until the harvest; and at harvest time I will tell the reapers, Collect the weeds first and bind them in bundles to be burned, but gather the wheat into my barn" (Matt 13:29–30).

The first intention is to protect the wheat: if you pull the weeds out, you could uproot the wheat, or think you're pulling weeds but pull wheat instead. Weeds disguise themselves as good plants all the time. This is a message for us—we can't always tell the difference between who's good and who's bad. The fact is that sometimes we're good and sometimes we're bad, but only God knows what we'll choose in the end. And this is the second intention; we might need a little time with some wheat to realize that we want to be wheat, too. Of course, in nature weeds can't become wheat, but in the human experience, we can—and God hopes that we will.

Miracles Are a Deeper Magic

Everything we need to make the world better has been given to us. It's up to us to take ownership of our abilities and responsibilities to make it happen. It comes down to free will: what I'm willing to do to be a force for good in the face of evil, and what I'm willing to remain apathetic or unresponsive to. It comes down to what I'm willing to sacrifice for the good of others.

In both *The Lord of the Rings* and the *Harry Potter* series, we see examples of people with great power sacrificing themselves to save the lives of those in their care. As mentioned previously, Gandalf fought the Balrog and lost his life. Dumbledore allowed himself to be killed by Severus Snape, a wizard pretending to be in the service of Voldemort. Snape, who had sworn to protect Harry, killed his friend Dumbledore at Dumbledore's own request as a means to save Harry's life. Only Harry could destroy Voldemort, and they were willing to sacrifice everything to give Harry his best chance.

This whole situation could have been easily handled if all the wizards remained faithful to the truth. They all knew what Voldemort was about. They all knew he was evil and that if he came into power, the world they knew would be altered in terrible ways. But motivated by fear, self-preservation, a desire for power, or whatever, they were willing to gamble that if they were faithful to a faithless one, he, who has no mercy, might be merciful to them and let them live.

Of course, they weren't really saving themselves; they were merely securing the preservation of mortal lives. How often and how easily we allow ourselves to believe that if we sacrifice the good of others, we'll somehow preserve it for ourselves. The sacrifice we offer is our best nature, making us slaves to a master who will never give us what we hope for. To reject our freedom to become slaves to things that prevent us from flourishing is to separate ourselves from our nature, from God's image.

In both the example of Gandalf and of Dumbledore, the sacrifices that they made secured the outcome of the quest that they were involved in. Gandalf was resurrected and made more powerful than before, and Dumbledore's spirit lived on as the spirits of wizards do. When we make sacrifices for others, we enlist a deeper magic—one that takes what we've done and multiplies it.

The Gospels are full of parables that talk about multiplying the joys of the kingdom of heaven. That kingdom has two meanings: one is actual heaven, God's domain where we live forever in indescribable joy and peace, and the other is God's reign on earth. There's a cool relationship between them: when we work for one, we accomplish the other. Jesus says that the kingdom of heaven is like a baker woman who adds yeast to flour, and it expands into a bunch of bread, or a tiny seed that grows into an enormous tree that birds live in (see Matt 13:31–33). Jesus showed us this truth in the multiplication of the loaves and fishes, when he took just a few loaves of bread and a little fish that people in his audience had with them and were willing to share. He blessed them, broke them, and gave them out, feeding five thousand people and even having leftovers (see John 6:1–13). Then, of course, when Jesus allowed himself to be killed by us, the effect of his death and subsequent resurrection multiplied exponentially to include anyone who wanted a part in it, bringing them eternal life. What God does isn't magical—it's miraculous.

Let's get a little more materialistic for a minute, because most of us don't have access to magic. Most of us *do* have access to at least *some* money, and money is a different kind of power. Bruce Wayne isn't a wizard (although he *is* a darn fine illusionist).

He's a man with a whole lot of money at his disposal. At a DC panel discussion at Comic Con, the question was asked, "If Bruce Wayne really cares about Gotham and stopping crime, why doesn't he use his wealth to bolster social services and fight crime at its roots?" It's a good question. Some would wonder if he refrains so he can stay in the Batman business. If everything was fixed, he'd be out of a job.

I've heard similar arguments against God by people who have the misconception that God's ego is fed by our subjugation to him. We know that God, being perfect within himself and needing nothing external, gains nothing from our worship, sacrifice, acceptance of his love, or anything else that we might offer. The answer is the same for both the question of Bruce Wayne's wealth and God's ultimate power; throw all the money/ power you want at a problem—if the individuals' hearts aren't changed, the problems will persist. Paying a villain off won't stop him; that's been proven every time their demands are met and they do what they threatened to do anyway.

Bruce Wayne does pour much of his money into social programs for the betterment of the poor and disenfranchised. God pours constant grace into his Church for the betterment of the poor and disenfranchised. But the effectiveness of programs and grace are contingent on the recipients' response to them. A Utopian society only works if everyone agrees to live by its ideals. God won't force us to be happy, and all the money in Bruce Wayne's estate won't fix the Rogue's Gallery. There will be darkness because humanity insists upon it.

Jesus said, "I am the light of the world. Whoever follows me will never walk in darkness but will have the light of life" (John 8:12). So, here's the thing; Jesus didn't eradicate the darkness that we'd have to endure in our lives, but gave us light to follow while we are immersed in the dark. The dark is always present. It's up to us as to whether we'll shine our light in it, or be swallowed up by it.

This image reminds me of two others; one is the phial that Galadriel gave to Frodo in Lothlórien, saying that it was to be used "as a light in dark places." She knew that Frodo's quest would take him into terrible physical darkness, but also into emotional desperation and near loss of hope in fearful situations while the evil of the Ring continued to work on him. The grace that Galadriel imparted with that gift didn't prevent him from experiencing darkness, but gave him what he needed as he entered the darkness to defeat it. The prophetic nature of her gift made it even more special. In 2 Peter 1:19, we hear, "So we have the prophetic message more fully confirmed. You will do well to be attentive to this as to a lamp shining in a dark place, until the day dawns and the morning star rises in your hearts." Whether we're amid difficulty or looking back on it in our past, our struggles have meaning when they're put into the larger context of faith.

The other image that comes to my mind is that of the Easter Vigil Mass on Holy Saturday. We enter a dark church that night, which represents the tomb of Christ. It's the terror that his followers were feeling—the loss that the planet felt (the Earth responded to Jesus's death with lightning, thunder, and earthquakes), the fear that we might experience when we believe that we're alone, the doubt that Jesus is who he says he is, and the worry that our efforts might come to nothing. But we enter that church, led by the paschal candle—an enormous candle that represents Jesus as the light of the world—and we all have our own candles lit from the paschal candle as we enter the darkness of the church, each of us sharing the light with the people around us. Before long, the church is lit with beautiful, flickering, soft warmth.

We're meant to take the light with us into the dark situations we encounter in daily life and bring that light to people who need it. We should be a beautiful, soft, warm oasis for those who hunger and thirst for beauty and comfort, like Galadriel for the Fellowship, like Dumbledore for Harry, like Jesus for the marginalized and hurting. It can be done in very small ways; as Saint Teresa of Calcutta told us, we can "Do small things with great love." Parents do it every day. First responders and medical personnel, the military, social workers, ministers, teachers—everyday people in every walk of life make a difference with their small acts of comfort and kindness that are done with great love.

It may seem like an unconventional example, but one who projects this image to me is Severus Snape. Snape wasn't known for being cuddly, sweet, soft, and warm. He was a professor at Hogwarts that most people didn't like, let alone trust. His specialty was the Dark Arts, which most felt fit his personality to a tee—he was dark, broody, and a loner. But what he did was truly done with great love—major league sacrificial love—especially because no one knew what he was about but him.

Snape, since his youth, had been in love with Harry Potter's mom, Lily. But although they were friends, she didn't consider him a romantic option and married his bully, James Potter, instead. When she and her husband were murdered by Voldemort, Snape committed himself to protect Harry out of his great love for Harry's mother. His choice to protect Harry meant that he would have to give up much. His actions had to be hidden from others, especially those who would tie themselves to Voldemort, so no one would suspect his mission. Among his colleagues and students, he gave the impression of being cold, hard, and uncaring. He treated Harry harshly so that there would be no inkling of his protection. Snape was entirely alone in his quest, which was truly thankless because no one knew to thank him. In the end, he made the hard choice to kill Dumbledore and die by the hand of Voldemort.

Snape's motivating love wasn't for Harry, or Hogwarts, or any friendships that he had. It was for Lily—a woman who didn't give him what he wished and hoped for. Her lack of reciprocation didn't daunt his love. He remained faithful without gaining anything in return, and his reward was a painful death. He created the circumstances necessary for Voldemort's destruction. But his love for Lily was so strong that it flowed out beyond Lily, defeating evil and saving the life that Lily valued most.

The deeper miracle of sacrifice and unconditional love is the reward of real, abundant life and an experience of true love. God's love for us and our charitable actions go far beyond what we can effect on our own. We should act for good because it is good, not because of anything we might gain for ourselves. It reminds us of the prayer of Saint Ignatius in which he asks God to help him do the good without counting the cost or seeking a reward. The divine irony is that the good we do is joined to the origin of good—God—and multiplied.

God won't come and fix everything for us, because we have been given what we need to do the job. We don't need magic to make things better. Most of the world's problems are caused by human sin. Take hunger, for example: there are enough resources on the planet for every individual to have a dignified quality of life, but we don't choose to implement them. That's not to say that you or I don't choose it. I can't think of a person who wouldn't want to stop the suffering of others...in theory. But what it would take to make it happen requires personal sacrifice. For most of us, that won't mean being killed for our beliefs, but it will mean choosing to let go of some comfort, wealth, maybe even a little bit of our security.

When God made us, he wove love into the fabric of our being. If there's any magic in us, it's that. Love can conquer all; it has the power to change people, destinies, outcomes of global events. Christians believe that Jesus is God's perfect revelation of his love, and we're supposed to model our behavior on his. We're told that "as many of you as were baptized into Christ have clothed yourselves with Christ" (Gal 3:27). It's our nature to be clothed in love and justice. If we embodied God's love, no force in the world could stop us.

CHAPTER NINE

FRODO AND SAMWISE

Our Pilgrim Church

One Is the Loneliest Number

We are a pilgrim people, always moving toward holiness and toward our final home with God in heaven. Our journey is often perilous and filled with adventure and mishap, and no one illustrates that journey better than Frodo and Samwise Gamgee in *The Lord of the Rings*. In their effort to save Middle-earth from the devastation of Sauron by destroying the Ring of Power, we're reminded that even those who are most resistant to corruption and discouragement need someone to lean on. We don't have to go alone. God gives us companions on the journey and sacred bread for strength. God made us in pairs (see Creation stories in Gen 1 and 2), sent the apostles out in pairs (Luke 10:1), and even gives us his own Spirit as a companion so that we're really never alone (Acts 2). Frodo and Sam had one another on their perilous journey, but even they needed help from some additional friends along the way.

Gamers know that "it's dangerous to go alone." When Link, the hero of the video game *The Legend of Zelda* (in its original incarnation), sets out on his quest to find the princess, Zelda (who is being held captive by the evil villain, Ganon), his first stop is a cave where he meets an old man. After the old man warns Link of the dangers of a lonely journey, he offers him a wooden sword, saying, "Take this." While a wooden sword is not very good company, and won't do very much damage to formidable foes, at least it was a start. The man was right—it *is* dangerous to go alone, and we do need help on our journeys.

We were made for community. Among the most prevalent problems in society today are feelings of loneliness and isolation, crossing all generations and demographics. Our mobile, wirelessly connected society brings us closer together, and simultaneously makes true intimacy a daily challenge. Unfortunately, many people seek intimacy, friendship, and a sense of belonging in pursuits that will isolate them even more. On one hand, I can feel the support of hundreds of friends and acquaintances when I post some struggle or grief on Facebook, and I might find some comfort in it. On the other hand, that comfort might serve as a lame substitute for one hearty conversation with a trusted friend that might have challenged me to look deeper, to grow, and to become stronger. I could begin to rely on social media numbers— only if I'm satisfied that I have worth or that my problem is understood, if I have enough "likes" or sad faces. Suicide is on the rise: it's the number three killer among preteens and young teens, and the number two killer in older teens and young adults. It can be traced to a lack of self-worth, not feeling loved, and the belief that they are alone.

Isolation is the tool of the enemy. People can become very desperate when they have no one to ground them, to call them back to reality. The most insidious thing about isolation is that it breeds more isolation. Feeling unloved and unwanted causes people to withdraw from others so that they don't feel rejection. Conversely, feeling superior and irresponsible to others makes people withdraw because nobody's worthy of their time or genius. But sometimes people need assistance in interpreting events and circumstances. If I relied entirely on what goes on in my own head to understand the world, I could come to some pretty messed up conclusions. I need to hear my thoughts out loud, to bounce them off people I trust to make sure I'm on the right track. If I don't, I set myself up as a god: infallible in my own thinking, an authority on everything. If anyone tries to challenge or correct me, even gently, I can freeze them out. I can become someone who's decided that I don't need anyone else's input. That's a fast track to becoming a supervillain.

The old phrase "safety in numbers" isn't just about physical safety—it's intellectual, emotional, and spiritual, too. I believe that isolation is the biggest joke that the devil ever played on humanity. I mentioned before that I believe that the disunity among Christians is the biggest tragedy in the Church. The more we split, the more we fracture, the weaker we become. The devil is having a field day with that. Each of us is convinced of our own correctness, not hearing the other, not learning from the other. That loner (and arrogant) stance cuts us off from the truth. Even children know that—when they want something they're not supposed to have, they'll divide and conquer their parents, playing them against one another.

Villains know it, too. If there's a strong hero group that can defeat them, their best bet is to sow discord in the group, turning them against one another. Although it was only in the movie, and not the books, in *Return of the King*, Gollum convinces Frodo that Sam has eaten all the lembas and can't be trusted. His lie was designed to separate the two, making Frodo more vulnerable and easier prey for Shelob, the giant spider Gollum tried to feed Frodo to. In the *Star Wars* franchise, Emperor Palpatine lied to Anakin Skywalker, who would later become Darth Vader, about his role in his own wife's death, as well as tricking him into believing that turning to the Dark Side was the only way to become powerful, save his wife, and fulfill his destiny. He convinced Anakin to forsake his mentor, Obi-Wan Kenobi, and to turn on the other Jedi, helping to hunt them down to destroy the Order.

Personal relationships and marriages break down because of a lack of communication, because of feelings of isolation, all the time. In Peter's first letter, sowing discord is listed among the worst sins: "But let none of you suffer as a murderer, a thief, a criminal, or even as a mischief maker" (1 Pet 4:15). In other translations, "mischief" appears as "intriguer." Intrigue sows doubt and suspicion among people, which breaks down trust and destroys intimacy. It breeds isolation. Beware instigators.

By contrast, having friends to work with on a common mission is paramount. It's why The Doctor always has a companion, superheroes have sidekicks, Captain Kirk has Spock and McCoy—every important hero has someone by their side at least from time to time. Many great stories begin with the forging of trusting friendships, without which the mission would fail. A fun example of this is the formation of the Voltron team. As with many successful hero groups, each comes from a very different background, bringing with them unique talents, baggage, foibles, and personalities. In the case of Voltron, there are five mechanical lions who are imbued with a kind of psychic sense. Like the rings of the Lanterns, the lions each choose their Paladin;

their pilot with whom they become linked. The lions are fierce fighting machines on their own, but they're in their most perfect form when they join to become Voltron, a humanoid robot and the most powerful weapon in the universe.

The only way that Voltron can be formed from the lions is if all five of the Paladins are working together—sharing in a unified vision, mission, and sense of team. Four of the five Paladins were only used to working alone, and they didn't especially like one another. Shiro, who would become the leader, as well as the head of Voltron (that is the *actual* head of the humanoid robot), had natural leadership skills and the ability to focus the group and help each to work together. When they had finally decided that they would do what it took to become a proper team, they found that the necessary unity would only come when each was looking out for the other, putting their teammates' safety above their own. They had to have each other's backs.

Once they figured that out, they could fight as Voltron, and as they grew together in trust and appreciation for one another's gifts, they became more powerful and efficient. If one tried to do something not in concert with the rest of the group, Voltron would fall; and I do mean literally fall, because Lance, whose lion makes one of the legs of Voltron, was always the one to go off script, which threw them off balance and tumbled the robot. Whenever that would happen, trust would be shaken and the team would be weakened (even if only for a moment). That problem brings home Paul's words:

> Indeed, the body does not consist of one member but of many. If the foot would say, "Because I am not a hand, I do not belong to the body," that would not make it any less a part of the body. And if the ear

would say, "Because I am not an eye, I do not belong to the body," that would not make it any less a part of the body. If the whole body were an eye, where would the hearing be? If the whole body were hearing, where would the sense of smell be? But as it is, God arranged the members in the body, each one of them, as he chose. (1 Cor 12:14–18)

As the members worked together, they grew in confidence, purpose, and their sense of personal value.

God created human beings in a pair for a reason. God wants us to have strong, fulfilling relationships because that's where we draw our strength and drive from. We hear in the second Creation story of Genesis that "the man said, / 'This at last is bone of my bones / and flesh of my flesh; / this one shall be called Woman, / for out of Man this one was taken.' / Therefore a man leaves his father and his mother and clings to his wife, and they become one flesh" (Gen 2:23–24). We're bound together by nature and by choice.

Throughout Scripture, God uses the image of a husband and wife for God's relationship with humanity to illustrate the intimacy that God wants for and with us. One of the most explicit examples is the Song of Songs (aka, The Song of Solomon). It's a love poem describing two lovers who are really into each other. He goes on about how beautiful she is, and she goes on about how she can't wait until they're together. It's meant to simultaneously express the romantic love between a man and a woman, but also the intimate, pining love that God has for us. When lovers are first in love, they want to spend all their time together. Eventually, things simmer down a bit and deep feelings and friendship occurs. If it progresses properly, each will try and put the needs of the other before their own; thus, the needs of each are fulfilled.

God's love for us never grows cold, and God wants us to want him as much as he wants us. God says, "Set me as a seal upon your heart, / as a seal upon your arm; / for love is strong as death, / passion fierce as the grave. / Its flashes are flashes of fire, / a raging flame. / Many waters cannot quench love, / neither can floods drown it. / If one offered for love / all the wealth of one's house, / it would be utterly scorned" (Song 8:6–7). Most people who have ever been in love can probably relate to that sentiment. God wants us to feel like that all the time, and to know that someone feels like that about us.

In a prayer attributed to Pedro Arrupe, SJ, who was the Jesuit superior general right after Vatican II, he names falling in love as the most important decision in our life: fall in love and stay in love, he says about God and others, and love will guide every single decision we make. This bond of love, when we choose it (just like human marriage), becomes a lifeline in every situation. In a good marriage, even when the spouses are apart, they are strength and inspiration for one another. They're never alone. It's the same with God: when we welcome God into our hearts, we're never alone. We have a companion on our journey in good times and bad, in sickness and in health, and so on. That relationship is one that carries us even if we might periodically feel like we're alone. In Catholic marriage, the vows are made between the man and the woman, but have God at the center. They're made publicly because the community is a witness to the vows, and are called upon in the liturgy to help the couple to live them fully.

Princess Buttercup and her betrothed, Westley, from *The Princess Bride*, shared "true love." The movie claims true love to be exceedingly rare—something that only happens once in a very long time, but everyone who saw Westley and Buttercup together knew that it was, without a doubt, true love. When she knew that her beloved Westley was alive after believing that he had been killed by the Dread Pirate Roberts, nothing could shake her faith in him. Even though the evil Prince Humperdinck told her that he had run away, and then later that he had died, she still believed that Westley would rescue her from the forced marriage that Humperdinck was trying to impose upon her. And Westley, even though he had been nearly killed, and was indeed, "mostly dead," found a way to get to his true love to save her from that terrible fate. Their love was so fierce and so pure that they wouldn't accept being apart as an option. As Westley says, "Death cannot stop true love. All it can do is delay it for a while." Paul the Apostle similarly says, "[Love] bears all things, believes all things, hopes all things, endures all things" (1 Cor 13:7).

Marriage isn't the only place where we know companionship and support. Jesus modeled the importance of friendship by gathering a small community around himself. Even though he was rightfully their master, he called them friends (see John 15:15). And when they were ready to go out and begin their mission of healing and proclaiming the good news to the world, he sent them out two by two. The story goes that "after this the Lord appointed seventy others and sent them on ahead of him in pairs to every town and place where he himself intended to go" (Luke 10:1). If they had split up they certainly could have covered more ground, but Jesus knew that they'd be more effective in pairs. Loneliness doesn't serve anyone well, and isn't

God's intention for anyone. Jesus says, "And remember, I am with you always, to the end of the age" (Matt 28:20).

A good friend can do wonders for a person...or a Hobbit.

Me for You, and You for Me

Let's circle back to one of the most famous, epic friendships there ever was, that of Frodo Baggins and Samwise Gamgee. When Frodo accepted the impossible task of taking the Ring of Power to Mount Doom to destroy it, he believed that he would have to go alone. Sam wouldn't hear of it, and no matter what danger came along, Sam stuck by Frodo's side. Sam made Frodo's mission his own mission, partly to save the world (or, more to the point, the Shire), and partly because of his love for, and sense of duty to, Frodo. There were times when Frodo didn't have the mental, emotional, or physical strength to go any further in his quest, and he had to rely on Sam's strength.

When the Fellowship was about to be formed, and a Ringbearer was to be chosen, Frodo volunteered. He felt that the Ring had come to his family for a reason, and it was up to him to remove it from Middle-earth. Gandalf the wizard and Elrond the Rivendell Elf agreed, in part, because Hobbits are especially resistant to evil. Frodo's uncle, Bilbo, had been in possession of and used it for a long time and, aside from feeling like he was "spread thin, like butter on too much bread," had not really been changed very much by it. Frodo showed a similar lack of corruption, so he had a pretty good shot at accomplishing its destruction. Yet, even with his Teflon Hobbit nature, Frodo was still affected by the evil it contained. There was no way that Frodo could ever had gotten to Mordor or destroyed the Ring on his own.

Other important friendships that supported the mission were formed as the stories developed. The Hobbits Merry and Pippin saved one another literally and figuratively throughout their journey. When they were parted, they formed even more friendships that furthered the mission—Pippin's presence in Minas Tirith saved the life of Faramir when his deranged father, Denethor, tried to have him burned alive. Merry's friendship with Éowyn helped get her to the battlefield where she killed the Witch-king of Angmar and turned the tide of the battle. If she hadn't been there, he wouldn't have been killed—no mortal man could kill him...but a *woman* could! And *did*! Legolas the Mirkwood Elf and Gimli the Dwarf, who should have been enemies according to the history between their people, forged an inseparable, friendly, competitive friendship that spurred each to be better in battle. And Legolas and Gimli together helped Aragorn to become who he needed to be by their faithfulness and support throughout the journey. All of them were working in different avenues to give Frodo and Sam the best chance they could have at getting the Ring to Mordor—each playing a part, each relying on the other.

As he and Sam were at the foot of Mount Doom, Frodo's burden had become too heavy for any one person to carry. It was in its master's realm, so its power grew, working against Frodo, challenging his resolve. The closer he got to the fires, the more unbearable the Ring became—it pulled toward its master in the Tower of Sauron, and since it had taken root in Frodo's heart, made him want to go, too. In his fatigue, he started to believe that he could keep the Ring for himself, and he knew he couldn't part with it. In the end, he didn't have the heart to destroy it because of its hold on him. But Sam did.

If Frodo had been alone, he certainly would have given up. He felt that, after carrying the Ring as long as he did, and the toll that the Ring and the journey had taken on him, there was no hope of him ever having any real peace if they ever got back to the Shire. Sam recalled the Shire for Frodo—everything about it that was important to save from the reign of Sauron—often bringing to mind stories of the Gaffer (his dad), the seasons, the countryside, and his plans. Sam's companionship called Frodo out of himself, helped him to see beyond the pain he was in from his hopeless feelings. Sam brought Frodo back to the reality of what was at risk if they didn't accomplish Frodo's task. Frodo's focus changed from what he could never have to what he might preserve for others. Using the last bits of their strength, Frodo and Sam made their way to the precipice. We might not rally for ourselves, but we will often rally for another. Having a companion and a loving community can be lifesaving. In saving someone else's life and soul, we just might be saving our own, too.

Frodo and Sam's mission was to save Middle-earth; ours is to save our Earth. God entrusted it to us, and told us to take care of it the way he would. Saving the world means making sure that everyone on it is valued, loved, cared for, and responsible to one another. No one should feel alone, and no one should not have their needs met. There's no reason for it with our societal advances. In the trailer for the movie *Transformers: The Last Knight*, Optimus Prime, the leader of the Autobots (good robots who have traditionally defended the Earth from the Decepticons, who are bad robots) is trying to destroy the Earth. A small band of dedicated humans and faithful Autobots, against all odds, are fighting to save it. Vivian Wembley, the adult heroine, reminds us, "When all seems lost, a few brave souls can save everything we've ever known." Izabella, a young girl who has joined the fight, says, "It's amazing what you can do when your life depends on it." Our lives *do* depend on it—our spiritual lives and the life of the world. And, it's as true in real life as it is in the movies—it can begin with a few brave souls—souls that stick together in common mission, fighting for their lives.

The soul of our planet is in danger. Although the world is smaller than ever thanks to technology that can bring us together in amazing ways, the world is lonelier than ever because we use it to hide our true hearts from one another. Each of us constructs the view that we want others to see; the media reports their version of truth that they would use to manipulate the masses; people are sharing more deeply personal things without any intimacy attached, leaving them feeling empty and more alone than they were before they put themselves out there; and we have been lulled into the myth that clicking "like" on a social justice story is "doing something" about it.

Human interaction is needed. True friendships with responsible sharing are needed. Relationships with real-world consequences are needed. Pope Francis speaks regularly about having personal encounters with the poor—not just throwing money at charitable agencies to ease our consciences, but spending time with people who are suffering. This is critical to saving the world because it humanizes the individual we are helping, and make us sensitive to the reality of their lives. I wouldn't let a family member or friend be homeless—I would do everything in my power to make sure that their needs were met. We're to make friends and family with the disenfranchised so that we have the same sense of responsibility toward them.

In the Book of Genesis, when Cain murdered his brother, Abel, in cold blood, God asked him where Abel was. Cain responded, "I do not know; am I my brother's keeper?" (Gen 4:9). Humanity continued to ask that question—Who is my neighbor? How do I deal with enemies? How often do I have to forgive my brother?—and was met every time with the same answer. Jesus was clear that everyone is beloved by God, is everyone else's responsibility, is as entitled to forgiveness as I am, and is worthy of our protection and love. He went so far as to say that, even when we hurt another person, it's as if we've killed them. "You have heard that it was said to those of ancient times, 'You shall not murder'; and 'whoever murders shall be liable to judgment.' But I say to you that if you are angry with a brother or sister, you will be liable to judgment; and if you insult a brother or sister, you will be liable to the council; and if you say, 'You fool,' you will be liable to the hell of fire" (Matt 5:21–22). God wasn't joking when he called us all sons and daughters, and told us that we were all brothers and sisters. Am I my brother's keeper? Yes. And we need to walk together.

Goal!

When Frodo and Sam finally finished the quest and the Ring was destroyed, it was time to go home. For Sam, that meant retiring to the Shire, marrying Rosie Cotton, and having some little hobbits. Frodo, however, couldn't return to his old life—he was too changed. Sam had been an excellent companion, but the toll that wearing the Ring took on Frodo made him too weary. Only the Elves could fully comprehend what that burden did to him. So, when they were finally ready to depart to the West (which represented heaven—really, it did: Tolkien was Catholic and spoke about his intended meaning behind the myth), they welcomed two additional passengers of the non-Elf persuasion, Bilbo and Frodo. Having been the two Ring-bearers who weren't totally corrupted by its evil, they were ready for a rest.

I'm always moved by the final scene in *The Return of the King*, when the Elves and Bagginses say their final goodbyes to Middle-earth. The Hobbit friends, Sam, Merry, and Pippin, are there to see them off. There are many tears and much sadness at the departure, but acceptance that it was time for Frodo and Bilbo to move from this life to the next. It makes me mindful of the goodbyes that we must make when someone we love goes home to God, and Jesus's words in the parable of the talents, "Well done, good and trustworthy slave; you have been trustworthy in a few things, I will put you in charge of many things; enter into the joy of your master" (Matt 25:23). Like the servant in the parable, Frodo took the hand he was dealt—an evil Ring he inherited, a dangerous quest he never expected—and invested himself to make a profit; in Frodo's case, to save the world. When he started out, he didn't realize that his final goal was anything other than the Shire by way of Mount Doom. He didn't realize that he was working toward heaven. Sometimes, it's the same for us.

Augustine of Hippo was another wanderer who set out on his convoluted journey, unsure of his destination for a good deal of his life. He didn't set out to save the world; he set out to party like it was 399, and party he did. He was a college kid who had no interest in his studies—he was there for the sex, drugs, and whatever the equivalent of rock 'n roll was at that time. His mother, Saint Monica, is famous for worrying about him, like any good mother would. But her worry wasn't devoid of action—

she prayed for her son furiously. Eventually, it paid off. Augustine got Jesus, got inspiration, got educated (for real), and got busy (in a good way). He became a doctor of the Church and is one of the most important teachers in Christian tradition.

One of his most famous quotes (and one of my favorites) is from his memoir, *Confessions*: "You have made us for yourself, O Lord, and our hearts are restless until they rest in you." Saint Augustine recognized that for a long time, he had been battling within himself. He knew he wanted something, but he didn't know what. He knew he was being drawn into something that would change him on an ontological level, but until he discovered that it was God he needed, he remained searching. He often found himself, as we all do, taking comfort in things that were sidetracking him from his purpose. Sin often masks itself to resemble the thing we want, but turns out to be as far from it as can be. Saint Augustine talks about looking for his purpose in love, which isn't off the mark, but the love that he was indulging in wasn't the love of God.

Food for the Journey

Frodo and Sam, the Paladins of Voltron, Cain and Abel, Link and Zelda, Westley and Buttercup, Saint Augustine, and everyone whom God ever created were made to be great heroes, but not in isolation. Factual or fictional, we're all made for an epic journey that will have an impact on the world we're in and the world we were created for. While the journey is full of danger, side-quests, failure, periodic successes, suffering, and joy, it's also meant to be shared. Each journey has a beginning and a destination. Our destination, our goal, is heaven. Our hearts are restless until they find their final home in God. We find moments of respite, support, intimate sharing, and growth because our relationships—both with God and other humans—nurture us. *The Lord of the Rings* is one of my favorite expressions of this relationship because of Tolkien's Catholic approach to journey. We've already explored the relationships among people in the stories, so let's look at the relationship with God.

It was woefully downplayed in the movies, but the Lembas bread that the Elves gave to the Fellowship had amazing qualities. In the book *The Return of the King*, Tolkien writes,

> The lembas had a virtue without which they would long ago have lain down to die. It did not satisfy desire, and at times Sam's mind was filled with memories of food, and the longing for simple breads and meats. And yet this waybread of the Elves had a potency that increased as travellers relied on it alone and did not mingle it with other foods. It fed the will, and it gave strength to endure, and to master sinew and limb beyond the measure of mortal kind.

That bread sustained their journey to the very end. It was no secret that Tolkien meant this to represent Eucharist; the bread that Catholics believe is changed to the body, blood, soul, and divinity of Christ in the sacrifice of the Mass. We call it "food for the journey." It's spiritual and physical nourishment that give us what we need to complete every major and minor quest that we're sent on. It's God's companionship with us, celebrated in the companionship of our faith community.

Lembas had the ability to restore the Hobbits, even healing them a bit from their wounds. It reminds me of the passage in Psalms: "He heals the brokenhearted, / and binds up their wounds" (Ps 147:3). The Eucharist heals our hearts and our bodies by strengthening our relationship with God and our community. We also say that Eucharist is the "foretaste of heaven," which we're told throughout Scripture resembles a wedding feast. That, of course, makes sense especially if you factor in the whole "God as spouse" theme throughout.

Every single person who was ever put on this Earth is precious to and beloved by God. Each of us is unique, called, and made for something great. We have stories to write and tell, communities in which to discover them, models to look up to and be inspired by, companions to brighten the dark times and share the load, intellect and will to inform our choices, freedom to pursue the justice that burns in our hearts, wounds that we can learn from and help others with, and connections with our Creator that help us to become more truly alive. The life that we've been gifted with is freely given, and has potential to be gift to our world. Choose companions who will help you to become the most authentic, free, courageous, fulfilled version of yourself that you can be, and yours will be a truly heroic life.

QUESTIONS TO PONDER

A Mentor's Nudge Builds a Hero's Life

As we conclude, let's consider a type of character we've met frequently on our journey: mentors. If there was no Alfred, there may not have been any Batman. If there was no Tick, Arthur would likely never have become the Moth that destiny had chosen him to be. If there was no Obi-Wan Kenobi or Yoda, Luke Skywalker would still be a whiney, blue-milk–drinking, droid-part–collecting brat. Everyone is born for greatness, but few would ever attain it without a little help from some friends. Where would the Ring's Fellowship be without Gandalf or Harry Potter without Dumbledore? The apostles were not doing anything particularly interesting before Jesus got ahold of them and invited them to follow him. But once they accepted that invitation, they became apprentices of the Master, and learned everything they would need to successfully complete the mission they had taken on.

Mentors offer a special relationship that helps us to see our assets, strengths, and shortcomings without telling us exactly how to use them. In the case of such heroes as Batman and Luke Skywalker, their mentors shared history with them and helped them to understand where they came from. They also illustrated the principles that the hero's parents embraced and upheld, why they were important, and how—if the hero chose to keep the tradition—their participation might affect the world (or galaxy). Their mentors offered them some direction—not a road map, not a detailed outline of their future decisions—but some wisdom to take wherever their path might lead them.

Christians apprentice themselves to Christ, living out our quests in the company of God's family, where we hear the history of our family, understand where we've come from, and are given an appreciation of where we're going. Each of us must discover, with the help of trusted guides, how to use our assets and strengths in the service of others, and how to improve on our shortcomings—and use *them* in the service of others.

Who are the mentors that help you to see yourself more clearly through the lens of God's loving eyes? What impact have mentoring relationships had on the choices you've made and the direction you've taken? How can you offer your wisdom in the service of others?

Questions to Consider

Introduction: Which Hero Are You?

1. Which heroes inspire you?

2. What not-so-super powers do you have to put in the service of others?

3. How will you live in a way that makes you more fulfilled and relevant?

4. Which of your tales will the bards sing of in the mead halls?

Chapter One: Super Groups: The Body of Christ

1. What community do you belong to that honors and encourages your gifts and talents?

2. What model of Church are you most comfortable with?

3. What do you gain from belonging to a community of faith?

Chapter Two: Superman and Aragorn: They're So Jesus

1. Which heroes speak most clearly to you of the person of Jesus?

2. What qualities in your favorite heroes are like those in Jesus?

3. How does mystery in the Christian sense invite you to a deeper reflection on your understanding of Jesus and his importance in your life?

Chapter Three: Batgirl: The Church in Democratic Nations

1. How do you see the work of the Church as countercultural?

2. What do you see as the place of faith in politics?

3. What are a couple of concrete ways that you can live justice in your daily life?

Chapter Four: Doctor Who: Breaking the Boundaries of Heaven and Earth

1. How do you experience the tension between the "already" and "not yet" of God's plan?

2. What does the continuity of God's love and care through-out salvation history tell you about God's care and plan for you?

3. What are some ways that you're "bigger on the inside"?

Chapter Five: The Lanterns: The Most Catholic of Superheroes

1. How responsible for your free will are you? How does knowing that it belongs to you make you more attentive to your reactions and responses?

2. What emotion or attribute are you most connected with? How does it affect the way you make decisions?

3. Do you ever have any dry periods, or desert experiences, of faith? How do you get through them?

Chapter Six: Villains: God's Not Done with Them Yet

1. What in your past could be content for a good supervillain backstory? What prevented it from becoming one?

2. What role does hope play in your life?

3. What are some experiences of forgiveness that you've had in your life? What impact did they have on your spiritual health and your outlook on life?

Chapter Seven: Batman: Wounded Healer

1. Who have been wounded healers for you?

2. How have your negative experiences come to be of service to you or others later on?

3. When you're wounded, where do you find your greatest healing?

Chapter Eight: Wizards: God's Not a Magician

1. Can you think of a time when you wished God would "just fix it"? Did you find a resolution?

2. Have you ever had an experience of answered prayer? Did it come the way you hoped it would?

3. How does the image of God as "lover" strike you? What would it mean in your life to live as if God were?

Chapter Nine: Frodo and Samwise: Our Pilgrim Church

1. Who have been your most important companions on your journey so far?

2. Do you see your Church community as suitable companions for you? If so, why? If not, what is lacking?

3. What role does Eucharist play in your journey? Do you find strength in God's gift of himself for you? Do you experience it as the intimate sharing that God intends it to be?